FROM ISOLATION TO CONVERSATION

SUNY Series, Teacher Preparation and Development
Alan R. Tom, editor

FROM ISOLATION TO CONVERSATION

Supporting New Teachers' Development

Dwight L. Rogers
and
Leslie M. Babinski

State University of New York Press

Published by
State University of New York Press, Albany

Printed in the United States of America

For information, address State University of New York Press, 90
State Street, Suite 700, Albany, NY, 12207

Production by Christine L. Hamel
Marketing by Michael Campochiaro

Library of Congress Cataloging-in-Publication Data

Rogers, Dwight L. 1948–
    From isolation to conversation : supporting new teachers' development
        / by Dwight L. Rogers and Leslie M. Babinski.
        p. cm.—(SUNY series, teacher preparation and development)
    Includes bibliographical references and index.
    ISBN 0-7914-5335-9 (alk. paper)—ISBN 0-7914-5336-7 (pbk.: alk.
    paper)
    1. First year teachers—In service training. 2. Teachers—In service training.
    I. Babinski, Leslie M., 1963- II. Title. III SUNY series in teacher preparation
    and development.

LB2844.1.N4 R63 2002   2001049460
371.102—dc21

                    10 9 8 7 6 5 4 3 2 1

To

New Teachers

and

Gail, Amy, and Nora,
And my parents Dwight and Virginia

and

Steve, Anna, and Katie
And my parents Paul and Barbara

Abstract

The first year in the classroom is an especially lonely and challenging time for many new teachers. This book is about our efforts to assist beginning teachers during this difficult period in their lives. The New Teacher Groups are an inquiry-oriented form of professional development that provides participants with the opportunity to engage in discussions with their peers about problems they are experiencing in their professional lives. By blending the fields of school psychology and teacher education, we adapted a consultee-centered consultation model to provide the framework for our approach. In this book we bring you real teachers voicing real problems encountered in real classrooms. We outline our process step-by-step so that the model can be adapted to help new teachers in many different kinds of school systems. Problem-based discussion groups like the New Teacher Group should be an integral part of any program designed to guide and support beginning teachers.

Contents

Contents

Acknowledgments

Writing a book, like filming a movie or staging a play, requires many dedicated and intelligent individuals working diligently behind-the-scenes. This book could not have been written without the help of the forty-nine teachers who participated in our New Teacher Groups. These teachers not only attended biweekly meetings during the school year but they also donated their precious personal time for one-on-one interviews and extended conversations about their first year in the classroom. Our colleague and friend Alan R. Tom provided us with the motivation to begin this project and was instrumental in providing a thorough and thoughtful critique of early versions of the book.

During our early days of writing we were extremely fortunate to have Mary Barnett working with us as a graduate assistant and New Teacher Group facilitator. Her organizational skills are unparalleled and she was steadfastly passionate about the potential of the New Teacher Groups for assisting beginning teachers. Jessica Durn's ability to catch the smallest of errors and to find the rarest of citations was a tremendous help to us in our push to complete our manuscript.

Finally, we are indebted to the thoughtful and creative assistance of Peggy Cronin, a gifted, encouraging, yet critical editor to whom we owe much, much more than just these few words of thanks.

Chapter 1

The First Year of Teaching

> **Rebecca, a third-grade teacher**: [Teaching is not what I expected!] Not at all! I guess I really expected it to be a lot more enjoyable than it has been. I know it has been rough because it is the first year. And it is always going to be rough in your first year. But I *never* expected it to be like this. I never thought I'd feel so down and so incompetent. It has been very difficult and I think a lot of it didn't have to happen. A lot of my grief and a lot of my uncertainties about myself as a person, about myself as a teacher, and about the teaching profession—I just don't think they were necessary . . . I have always been a go-getter and throughout the year I [have] always continued to do my best. But there have been times this year when I felt so small that I couldn't even scrape myself off of the floor.

False expectations, shattered dreams, and serious attacks on one's competence and self-worth—these are the all too common experiences of beginning teachers. Teaching is a demanding and at times debilitating job that requires extraordinary expertise in human relations, tremendous organizational abilities, profound patience, and the wherewithal to make hundreds of situation-specific decisions over the course of a school day. And, as Rebecca so vividly illustrates by her comments, the first year of teaching is often an especially trying and even traumatic time for those new to the profession.

1

The Challenges of Teaching

For more than a quarter of a century much has been written about the myriad problems new teachers face in their initial year in the profession (Bell & Gilbert, 1994; Bullough, 1987; Feiman-Nemser, 1983; Fuller, 1969; Grant & Zeichner, 1981; Kestner, 1994; Ryan, 1970; Veenman, 1984). Yet despite all of the research and all of the books and articles written about the difficulties endured by beginning teachers, the first year of teaching continues to be an exceptionally difficult time for most of them.

Even experienced teachers find it challenging to meet the diverse needs of children in today's classrooms as well as to complete all the many administrative and curricular tasks assigned to them. Yet beginning teachers—who are often ill prepared for the emotional, physical, social, and psychological demands of teaching (Huling-Austin, 1990)—are thrust into their own classroom with few materials and little or no administrative or collegial assistance. Among the biggest obstacles faced by these teachers are the deep sense of isolation and a lack of real community (Ashton, 1984) along with the all too quick transition from student to teacher (Lieberman & Miller, 1984).

The Culture of Isolation
The physical and social isolation suffered by most teachers has long been a problem in the teaching profession and continues to create significant difficulties for teachers today (Goodlad, 1984; Johnson & Pugach, 1996; Lightfoot, 1983; Lortie, 1975). Opportunities for teachers to engage in genuine professional dialogue are rare in the schools. Both the design of most school buildings and cultural-historical norms of schooling encourage little if any professional, and even personal, interaction among teachers (Goodlad, 1984; Lightfoot, 1983; Lortie, 1975). Britzman (1986) points out that in addition to the physical structures that inhibit interaction in schools, there are invisible walls constructed by the "culture of teachers" that perpetuate a lack of community. It is this "culture of teachers," which promotes privacy and autonomy, which establishes barriers to genuine dialogue among teachers in schools. The value schools place on self-reliance also imposes what Lieberman and Miller (1984) call the "rule of privacy," under which it is permissible to talk about the weather and sports or to "complain in general about school and the students," while it is unusual for teachers to talk to each other about teaching and about the details of what goes on in their classrooms (p. 11).

Transition Shock

In addition to working in a school culture that expects teachers to handle their own problems, there is an unrealistic expectation that all new teachers should have the ability to assume the role of expert from day one (Lortie, 1975). In no other profession do we expect those new to the field to perform the same tasks at the same level of competence as those with years of experience. This expectation is played out each fall as new teachers time and time again shoulder the same responsibilities as their more experienced colleagues.

A result of this rapid assumption of responsibility is that beginning teachers move quickly from the "fantasy stage" to the "survival stage" where they are "fighting" for their professional lives (Ryan, 1986, p. 13). Given the multiple demands of teaching and the unrealistic expectations for new teachers, it is no wonder that these teachers experience what Corcoran (1981) refers to as "transition shock." This shock, suffered by new teachers in the abrupt transition into the profession, can be attributed to their often idealistic and naive mental models of teaching, models that are radically different from the reality they are suddenly experiencing (Glassberg, 1979; Hawk, 1984; Odell, 1989; Ryan, 1986). Leiberman and Miller (1984) claim this sudden transition from college student to class-room teacher leaves the novice alone "with degree in hand, high expectations internalized, a fistful of untried methodologies, and few adults with whom to share, grow, and learn" (p. 4).

It is not at all surprising that only about 50 percent of the new teachers' careers last longer than five years (Gordon, 1991; Huling-Austin, Odell, Ishler, Kay, & Edelfelt, 1989). According to a recent analysis of federal survey data by *Education Week*, one in five teachers leave the profession after three years; those who score in the top 25 percent of the SAT or ACT are more likely to leave (Cooper, 2000). The attrition rate is more pronounced in some districts where as many as 40 percent resign before their second year (Wise, Darling-Hammond, & Berry, 1987). According to Bullough (1987), many of the teachers who remain in classrooms end up teaching in ways that are inconsistent and even contradictory to their initial pedagogical beliefs, goals, and expectations.

The Critical Nature of the First Year of Teaching

The lack of teacher-to-teacher dialogue in schools impacts the morale and even discourages the professional growth of experienced teachers. The lack of opportunity for collegial conversations may have even greater implications for beginners who are in the earliest and most vulnerable stage of professional development (Veenman, 1984). The literature on teacher development suggests that the process of becoming a teacher does not cease at the end of formal training; rather it continues into the induction year and beyond (Levin & Ammon, 1992). The literature further indicates that the first year of teaching is important in setting the stage for later growth. According to Thies-Sprinthall (1986), "initial learning experiences in new and emotionally charged situations often have the quality similar to an indelible imprint" (p. 14). Still others believe that the early years are *the* most critical time in a teacher's career (Grant & Zeichner, 1981). In other words, the first years in teaching form the "connection between the former and future experiences" (Hopkins, 1996, p. 29).

While the induction years function as the formative period for learning how to teach, they are equally important as a time for beginners to gain a clearer, deeper understanding of themselves as teachers. Gregorc and Ward (1977) call the first year the "becoming stage" and they believe this to be the critical period in which an initial model of teaching is formed. Bush (1965) claims that the first years are when a new teacher learns her "role, internalizes the basic values of the teacher's culture," and also forms the foundation for his or her beliefs about teaching—beliefs that will impact their actions both in the present and the future (p. 7). Feiman-Nemser (1983) emphasizes the importance of the first years in the teaching profession:

> Various labels (induction phase or transition phase) have been used to signal the fact that the first year of teaching has a character of its own, that it is different from what has gone before and likely to influence what is to come. Some go so far as to argue that what happens during the first year of teaching determines not only whether someone remains in teaching but also what kind of teacher they become. (pp. 157 -158)

The unique nature of the experience of beginning teachers strongly suggests the need to move beyond the traditional skill-oriented workshop approach as their primary mode of support. It also implies the need to seriously consider how we can provide support for beginners during this trying time in their lives, while also encouraging them to cultivate a clearer conception of themselves in their new role as teachers. In the next section we discuss our New Teacher Groups as a powerful way to provide a different type of professional development for beginning teachers.

Moving Beyond the Workshop Approach

Teaching is a complex and demanding activity that requires the generous social and emotional support of others in the profession. Traditional methods of assistance and professional development often fall short of meeting the pedagogical and personal needs of beginning teachers. Teachers are seen as passive recipients of knowledge in the traditional workshop model, where the emphasis is on the "how" of teaching rather than on the "who" or the "why" (Banner & Cannon, 1997). New teachers frequently complain that the standard induction model of professional development provides the wrong kind of information at the wrong time and in the wrong way. The implicit message communicated by this form of professional support is that teaching is a simple, straightforward, and overly mechanistic activity (Lieberman & Miller, 1999; Meyer, 1999). This kind of professional training imputes that learning how to teach requires only that beginners accumulate a variety of techniques and skills—skills seen as so simplistic that they can be learned in afterschool workshops. In this workshop format and in other traditional forms of professional development, teachers are seen as technicians who are only expected to "carry out orders from above [and then] are deprived of the occasion to bring to bear on their work the whole of their intelligence, understanding and judgment" (Duckworth, 1994, p. 16). In addition to oversimplifying and degrading the work of teachers, Meyer (1999) suggests that "this unidirectional mode of professional development can teach novice teachers that their own ideas, questions, and concerns about teaching are not valued" (p. 13).

Although we do not disagree that new teachers need to improve their teaching skills, we think they also need much more. What is missing from most skill-oriented professional development approaches is the chance for these teachers to talk to other new teachers—the opportunity to reflect on their work by engaging in earnest and sustained conversations about teaching with their peers. Gilroy (1989) contends that the problem with the traditional hierarchical, skill-oriented model of induction is that it "savagely narrows the vision" of the beginning teacher and makes "alien the conception of self-reflection" as a form of knowledge (pp. 107, 110). New teachers need opportunities for discussions with other teachers if they are to be effective in the classroom in their first year and in years to come. In fact, Meyer (1999) claims,

> Regardless of the labels affixed, successful professional develop-
> ment practices center on two main qualities. First, that teachers
> develop professionally when they meet to learn and deliberate
> about and from experience. Equally important, all of these col-
> laborative occasions for professional development revolve around
> teachers talking together. (p. 39)

It is through collaborative conversations with colleagues that new teachers begin to ask who they are and inquire more seriously into what kind
of teachers they want to become (Harris, 1995; Hollingsworth, 1992;
Meyer, 1999). Featherstone, Munby, and Russell (1997) point out that
new teachers often "sell themselves short," and that providing them with
opportunities to talk and develop their own "voice can counter this
tendency" (p. 3).

Given the fact that traditional forms of professional development
(which focus on discrete techniques and skills) do little to relieve the
effects of isolation or to enhance beginning teachers' understanding of
themselves or their craft, the question then is, How can we support the
development of these teachers in ways that respect them as competent and
capable professionals who still have much to learn about teaching and
about themselves as teachers? One method for supporting the professional development of new teachers is described in this book.

New Teacher Groups
As a former elementary teacher and a school psychologist, we were well
aware of the incredible demands and the high level of stress most people
experience in their first-year of teaching. Our concern for improving the
first-year experience for beginning teachers was rooted in compassion for
the suffering they endure in their initial years in the profession. We also
had a sincere interest in providing these teachers with genuine opportunities to learn and to develop their professional selves. As we have already
suggested, the initial years are crucial times to not only support but also
challenge new teachers' ideas and practices.

We wanted to provide these teachers with a "safe space" (Lieberman
& Miller, 1984) for engaging in collaborative conversations about their
teaching and about their lives as teachers. We wanted to provide a place
where they could voice their concerns, share their joys and frustrations,

and work to assist one another in better defining and addressing their problems and issues—a place where they could grow professionally. We believed we could do this by designing a setting where teachers would have the opportunity to engage in genuine professional dialogue with their colleagues. Thus, in 1995 we decided to create a group that offered new teachers a regularly scheduled time to talk honestly and openly with their peers about their experiences in schools and about the problems they confronted daily in their work. Between 1995 and 1998, a total of forty-nine teachers participated in one of nine New Teacher Groups that met every other week throughout the school year. All the group sessions were audiotaped and the teachers were interviewed individually at the end of the year about their teaching and about their experience in the groups.

Book Overview

This book tells the story of our New Teacher Groups and of the teachers who participated in them. We begin by explaining the rationale for providing elementary teachers with a different kind of professional development. Next, we describe the theoretical framework we followed in our New Teacher Groups and outline our research methods and the format we adopted for our group meetings. In the second half of the book we elaborate on the findings from our study of beginning teachers who participated in our groups.

Whenever possible we allow the teachers to describe their experiences of their first year in the classroom and their perceptions of the New Teacher Groups in their own words. In order to protect the group participants' confidentiality, we use pseudonyms for each teacher and make no references to specific places. This book is filled with the voices of new teachers—teachers like Rebecca, a third-grade teacher, Craig, a fifth-grade teacher, and Loretta, a third-grade teacher.

Rebecca taught in a small town located in a rural county in the South, a town that has a history of thorny race relations between African-American and white citizens. It is now in the midst of a tremendous influx of Latino/Latina immigrants. This new demographic is transforming the social and cultural landscape, the politics of which are being played out in the elementary school. Rebecca, like so many of the new teachers in our groups, is a dynamic and well-educated white woman in her early twenties. She recently graduated from a respected college with a degree in elementary and early childhood education and soon after moved hundreds of miles from the Midwest to the South to accept her first teaching position.

Another new teacher in one of our groups, Craig, received a full scholarship to a state university in exchange for a commitment to teach in public schools for at least four years. In this part of the South, it is still a little unusual to see a twenty-two-year-old white male college graduate teaching elementary schoolchildren. Craig landed his first job teaching fifth grade only a few miles from the college he attended. The school, located in an old cow pasture miles from any development, serves African-American and white students whose socioeconomic backgrounds range from rural poor to suburban wealthy. Craig is an especially thoughtful, well-read, articulate, and likable person who had excellent rapport both with his students and with the other teachers at his grade level. However, despite the support Craig received from the other fifth-grade teachers and his principal, there were many situations in which he was unsure of what he should do and felt like there was no one at school to help him. In spite of his generally supportive teaching environment, Craig found that he too needed to talk regularly with his peers to help him work his way through the difficulties of the first year.

Another teacher, Loretta, volunteered to participate in an experimental elementary teacher education program as an undergraduate student in a highly respected university. She was one of only two African-American women out of the thirty students enrolled in this program. Like Rebecca and Craig, Loretta was confident, intelligent, and well prepared to teach. Her first year was spent teaching third grade in an elementary school that served mostly middle- and lower-income white and African-American students. The school is located in a small town that is transitioning quickly from what was once a rural farm town to a bedroom community for larger cities in the region. Loretta found that there were teaching issues that her colleagues at school and her friends and family were not interested in or willing to discuss. What seemed like an unflappable and confident exterior sometimes crumbled when Loretta spoke about some of the problems she was facing at school.

Rebecca, Craig, and Loretta, like most of their peers, were bright, articulate, motivated, well prepared, and determined to be good teachers. Yet nonetheless, their first years of teaching were on the whole unnecessarily difficult, stressful, and at times even painful. In the chapters that follow you will hear more from Rebecca, Craig, and Loretta, plus from many of the other teachers who participated in our group meetings.

In chapter 2, we provide the rationale for offering teachers a different kind of professional development opportunity. In chapter 3, we describe the workings of problem-based discussion group meetings and present the theoretical framework we used to organize, structure, and facilitate meetings. In chapter 4, we present our guiding questions, describe the methodology used to analyze our data, and outline our findings on the types of issues new teachers discussed. Our summary of the benefits of participating in a New Teacher Group are based on the analysis of our interviews with the participating teachers and are reported in chapters 5 and 6. In chapter 7, we describe the structural features of the New Teacher Groups that contributed to our ability to assist beginning teachers with their problems and to encourage the development of their understanding of teaching and of themselves as teachers. Finally in chapter 8, we present a summary of our key findings and broaden the discussion to include other elements in a comprehensive induction program for beginning teachers.

Chapter 2

A Different Kind of Professional Development

> **Victoria, a fifth-grade teacher**: [The group] was a really nice source of support that I could not have found here [at my school] only because there were not enough first-year teachers to do that with. It was support that could not come from anywhere else except from people in exactly the same boat as myself.

The opportunity to share joys and frustrations with others who are experiencing similar issues cannot be overemphasized. Fessler and Christensen (1992) argue that since lifestage theories all stress the importance of transitional periods of change or turning points in the lives of adults, we must carefully consider how to best assist beginning teachers in this especially difficult and sensitive time in their lives. They contend that a quality professional development program must address the new teachers' need for security, affiliation, and self-esteem if it is to really help them become competent and caring teachers. In this chapter we discuss the features of collaborative learning communities that address these needs.

Important Features of Collaborative Learning Communities

The primary difference between "professional-development-as-usual" (Meyer, 1999) and collaborative learning communities is the emphasis on

11

peer interaction. Shulman (1999) highlights the importance of a community in learning and states, "Learning flourishes when we take what we think we know and offer it as community property among fellow learners so that it can be tested, examined, challenged, and improved before we internalize it" (p. 12). We, too, believe that a community is important for learning.

The Need for Peer Support

Research on social support networks provides us with insights on how to help newcomers to the profession cope with especially stressful periods such as the first year of teaching (Tellez, 1992). For example, Caplan (1974) suggests that the stress resulting from the social and psychological disorientation of a new job is magnified when feedback is either missing or conflicting. Tellez believes that the isolation teachers suffer in schools prevents them from acquiring the feedback necessary to help relieve some of their stress. He insists, therefore, that it is crucial for new teachers to "form a social network to alleviate stress and disorganization" (p. 215). Likewise, Gottlieb (1988) contends that the social and emotional needs of beginning teachers may not be well served through traditional workshops or even through mentoring programs but through the formation of a community of learners. According to Gottlieb, "as much as people need the emotional intimacy of a single confidante, they also need a sense of a reliable alliance with a set of valued peers" (p. 23).

The results of research on teacher induction into the profession strongly suggest the need to provide first-year teachers with frequent opportunities to share experiences and solve problems collaboratively (Huling-Austin, 1992). Sprinthall and Theis-Sprinthall (1983) found that adults are more likely to learn when they have the opportunity to interact with peers. This is corroborated by Schlechty (1984) who maintains that groups for beginning teachers may reduce isolation while fostering professional growth. Schlechty feels that creating groups exclusively for new teachers is important because it allows them to know that others, too, are experiencing similar difficulties and stress in their work. He also believes that beginning teacher discussion groups can help these teachers develop a sense of belonging by sharing their ordeals.

Because these new teachers were all going through similar experiences, they had much to share with one another. We thought that frequent opportunities to talk seriously about their work with other new teachers could provide a vehicle for community building. Below, Meyer (1999) outlines four important points describing the potential value of community membership:

> (1) Belonging to a community of peers can offer novice teachers social, emotional, and intellectual balm for the rigors of teaching, (2) established teacher communities develop an inquiry culture focused on the dilemmas of practice, allowing teachers to learn from experience—their own and the experience of others, (3) though not an end in and of itself, participation in an inquiry-based community of peers can help teachers gain a better understanding of and capacity to foster student learning, and (4) in order to learn from experience, teachers must have access not only to a community that engages in inquiry but to a community that has the capacity to talk in certain productive ways. (p. 7)

Like Meyer (1999), we felt that we could begin to ease the sense of isolation that new teachers experience in their schools by creating a community of peers in which these teachers could talk about their work. We wanted teachers to realize that, despite their early experiences in the teaching profession to the contrary, there are other educators upon whom they could depend and trust to help them with their problems. In accordance with Pierce's and Gilles's (1993) ideas about what is learned through dialogue, we also believed that through conversation we could "learn about one another and begin to trust each other," and furthermore this trust enables us "to establish and sustain learning communities" (p. ix).

The value of engaging in problem-solving within a community of peers has been supported by the work of other scholars (Bakhtin, 1981; Brufee, 1993; Harris, 1995; Hollingsworth, 1992; Vygotsky, 1978). Brufee (1993) argues that learning is a collaborative enterprise where knowledge is constructed by negotiation through conversations in communities of knowledgeable peers. Vygotsky (1978) claims that dialogue provides a powerful vehicle for learning and development. Vygotsky further asserts that individuals learn and develop from the outside in, or in other words, individual development moves from the interpersonal to the intrapersonal.

Like Vygotsky (1978), Bakhtin (1981) writes persuasively about the power of a community in stimulating individual growth. Bakhtin maintains that our personal, or "inside," voice(s) and our social, or "outside," voice(s) exist simultaneously as a result of, and at the expense of, each other. As we engage in dialogue, we call upon and respond to both "the others without" and to "the others embedded within." It is this tension between the personal and the social that Bakhtin believes stimulates the conversations that are absolutely essential for intellectual growth. In addition to Meyer (1999), Harris (1995), and Hollingsworth (1992), we strongly suggest that there is great potential for supporting new teachers through the creation of dialogic communities where teachers seriously discuss the problems and dilemmas confronting them in their daily work.

The Importance of Dialogue

Dialogue is a process that is concerned with developing self, getting to know others, and forming human relationships (Matson & Montagu, 1967). Dialogue encourages the possibility for collaboration because it is a "humanizing speech" that lacks prescription and "challenges and resists domination" (Collins, 1991, p. 212). "Dialogue is characterized by high levels of concern for self (and one's own position) as well as for the other (and the position advanced by the other.) In dialogue, one must stand up for one's self and one must care about the other" (Cissna & Anderson, 1994, p. 14). Because dialogue encourages us to focus on ourselves and others within the same activity, it can simultaneously promote the development of self and enhance a sense of commitment to others. Thus it carries with it the potential for encouraging personal confirmation and the creation of community.

Dialogue is powerful because it not only connects individuals and ideas, it also stimulates change. Cissna and Anderson (1994) suggest that dialogue is much more than a simple back-and-forth exchange of information through verbal interaction. In fact, they insist that dialogue "points to a particular process and quality of communication in which the participants 'meet,' which allows for changing and being changed" (p. 10). They contend that participating in dialogue can stimulate change both among and within individuals, because in dialogue "we have not 'planned' what we will say or who we will be" (p. 24). Furthermore, Cissna and Anderson believe that through dialogue "we become most fully ourselves, we realize ourselves most deeply, as we respond to the call of the other" (p. 24).

Other researchers make equally strong claims for the power of dialogue in supporting the professional growth of teachers. According to Cochran-Smith and Lytle (1993), teachers construct fresh insights into their practice by engaging in deep discussions centered around the thoughtful analyses and interpretations of events experienced in their schools and classrooms. Hollingsworth (1992) contends that collaborative conversations contain the social interaction and intellectual stimulation that encourage new teachers to (a) gain "power to think and act within an uncertain framework," (b) more easily locate resources and develop personal support systems, (c) "create and analyze broader knowledge about teaching," (d) "better identify" with the struggles of children having difficulty learning, and (e) adopt a "feminist challenge to traditional concepts of learning to teach" (pp. 398-399). Sergiovanni (1994) and Shulman (1988) claim that teachers' roles as learners in collaborative discussions with their peers seem to inspire them to teach in more innovative and sophisticated ways. More generally, Corcoran (1995) states that teacher engagement in genuine dialogue around such issues as teaching, curriculum, evaluation, and assessment fosters professional development. Richert (1992) asserts that it is critical that we provide beginning teachers with opportunities to converse with other teachers because they

> learn to think as they talk, and they become conscious of what they know and believe as they hear themselves speak (and examine what they've spoken). . . . Listening to yourself as an authority on your own experience . . . is an important part of learning. In fact listening to your own words and attempted explanations is fundamental to reflective practice that results in learning to teach. (p. 193)

The Value of Personal Narratives

Typically teachers engage in dialogue about their teaching by sharing their stories and responding to the stories of other teachers. Genuine dialogue is valuable because it "forces" us to think and to listen, thus allowing us to come up with new ideas while encouraging us to think about things in ways we have never thought before.

The stories that teachers tell usually focus on their students and their lives as teachers. These teacher narratives do more than just assist teachers in communicating with each other; their stories provide a powerful vehicle for engaging others—as a means to share and to better understand their own experiences (Gomez & Tabachnick, 1992). As Noddings and Witherell (1991) write, "we learn from stories. More important, we come to understand—ourselves, others, and even the subjects we teach and learn" (p. 279). In fact, Bruner (1986) identifies storytelling as a critical mode of human thought. MacIntyre (1981) further suggests that actions become intelligible when people tell others about their intentions and that certain kinds of narratives are the "basic and essential genre for the characterization of human actions" (p. 194). Along these same lines, Friedman (1993) maintains that in certain contexts "stories give coherence to people's experiences" and involve "intentions and feelings" (p. 201). He continues by stating that "narratives reflect a discrete mode of thought, evidenced by how we impose a narrative structure on human experiences and how stories capture our attention" (p. 201).

Harris (1995) contends that sharing personal stories with others helps new teachers better understand "who they are" because "constructing personal narrative helps us to organize and make sense of our lives, and in the process, helps us make sense of who we are, have been, and might become" (p. 15). She goes on to explain that sharing personal narratives is particularly valuable for teachers because

> Through the telling and hearing of stories . . . people learn about themselves and others. . . . Telling a story to someone else puts us in touch with what we know and are coming to know, while at the same time, lets us step back from that knowing in order to reflect upon it, to "look over our own shoulder," so to speak. But telling stories does more than simply help us understand and reflect upon our lives. The personal narratives we tell ourselves and others actually come to structure how we perceive information and experiences, and ultimately determine the way we organize and make sense of our world, thus shaping our personal and professional identities. (p. 16)

New Teacher Groups

The framework that we followed in our New Teacher Groups encompasses each of the principles just described. This model, based on Caplan's consultee-centered consultation theory (1993), is particularly well suited for encouraging problem solving through dialogue and reflection and, in the process, facilitating the professional growth of new teachers.

To summarize thus far, it is clear that the first year of teaching is a continuous struggle for many new teachers, as illustrated by Rebecca, a third-grade teachers who said, "I *never* expected it to be like this. I never thought I'd feel so down and so incompetent . . . there have been times . . . I've felt so small that I couldn't even scrape myself off of the floor." Like Rebecca, many teachers experience an extremely stressful, discouraging, and disorienting first year. Although we hoped to advance professional development by creating the New Teacher Groups, we also felt an especially urgent need to simply help beginning teachers cope with the reality of their jobs and their lives as teachers.

Resilience has become a popular term to denote the ability to overcome some type of risk. The concepts of risk and resilience can be useful in thinking about how to best provide support for new teachers. The stress on new teachers is not only personally debilitating but also serves as risk factors that impact the effectiveness of one's teaching and eventually lead to burnout and even to leaving the profession.

We believe that collaborative conversation groups have the potential to provide the kind of support necessary to help teachers become more resilient to the stress they constantly endure in their work. Although we do not believe that New Teacher Groups alone can solve all the problems facing new teachers, it is clear that the opportunity to engage in discussions about their work with peers can have a profound effect on these teachers' understanding of their own teaching and of themselves as teachers.

We will now describe the workings of the New Teacher Groups in detail. We describe the method of group consultation that provided a valuable organizing structure and a group-process approach that served to stimulate dialogue through problem solving in our New Teacher Groups. We will then describe our research methods, provide a demographic description of the teachers who participated in the New Teacher Groups from 1995 to 1998, and present the types of problems and issues that the teachers discussed in the groups over those three years.

Chapter 3

Description of Our New Teacher Groups

> **Maria, a first-grade teacher**: The most helpful [thing about the group] was the . . . way we structured it . . . and the way that after we went around and told something positive then everybody focused on those people that had the most pressing problems at the time . . . [The facilitators] were really handy because they were always there to pull us back and say "OK, but this is the issue at hand" so we didn't just turn the group into a complaining session. We were there for a purpose and there was a structure to it.

We created the New Teacher Groups in order to provide beginning teachers with regularly scheduled opportunities to engage in professional dialogue with one another in a place where they could talk safely about their issues and concerns. As the new teachers realized that they were not the only ones having difficulty in their first year, they drew strength from the group and were able to see their issues from multiple perspectives. The overall goal for these groups was to provide these teachers with the chance to share their successes and failures, raise questions and concerns, and in the process provide each other with much-needed social and emotional support. It was clear from the research literature that dialogue was a powerful medium for communication and that much could be learned both personally and professionally by creating opportunities for extended discussions around issues of immediate importance to new teachers.

Through collaborative problem solving in the groups, first-year teachers helped each other define, understand, and even begin to address their pedagogical, curricular, interpersonal, and political concerns. This problem-posing and problem-solving process could not only create a mechanism where teachers would rally around each other for support but also would encourage reflection and a richer understanding of their own teaching.

In an attempt to provide a structure that facilitated collaborative discussions among the new teachers in the group, we adapted the problem-solving process from Caplan and Caplan's (1993) consultation theory. This consultation process provided a framework for our discussions that helped the new teachers cope with their situations in a way that would foster personal and professional learning and growth.

In this chapter we provide a detailed look at the structure and process we used to guide the discussions in our New Teacher Group meetings.

Consultation

Our New Teacher Groups created professional relationships that were unlike most others that teachers encountered in their schools. The group facilitators had no supervisory or evaluative power over the teachers, nor did they have any responsibility for the students in the teachers' classrooms. Because of the unique nature of this relationship, we decided to follow a consultee-centered consultation approach that focused on the teacher's professional development. (The teacher is called the "consultee" in this approach.) The primary focus of consultee-centered consultation is on helping the teacher become a more effective professional. In this approach, the main objective is to improve the teacher's capacity to deal with a current problem and future similar problems (Caplan & Caplan, 1993). Since it was clear from the research literature that the initial focus of the teacher is inward (i.e., on herself as a teacher), we felt that a consultee-centered model was an appropriate choice to guide our New Teacher Groups.

Caplan's model of consultation has been used to support professional development in a number of diverse disciplines; Caplan describes his use of consultee-centered consultation with nurses, rabbis, social workers, and judges (Caplan & Caplan, 1993). The benefits of this type of approach for educators have been described (Caplan, Caplan, & Erchul, 1995), although our study is the first that we know of that systematically uses Caplan's consultation framework for supporting beginning teachers during the induction phase.

Given the difficulties faced by these teachers and by the lack of a collaborative culture in many schools, Caplan's model of consultation is an effective way to address these needs. According to this consultation approach, learning and generalization are more likely to occur when the teachers are in control (Brown, Pryzwansky, & Schulte, 1998). Furthermore, consultation has been found to improve teachers' problem-solving skills, facilitate teachers' understanding of, and attitude about, children's problems; and promote gains in long-term academic achievement (Meyers, 1995). We hoped that helping the new teachers become more effective professionals would positively impact their students, not only in current classrooms, but also for years to come.

Caplan's model of consultation is ideal for supporting beginning teachers because it focuses on the noncoercive nature of the consultant-consultee relationship and on the need for a collaborative dialogue to foster orderly reflection (Caplan, Caplan, & Erchul, 1995). The first of these elements, the noncoercive relationship, is especially important in a group setting with beginning teachers who are in a vulnerable position and very sensitive to evaluative comments by parents, administrators, and other teachers. By establishing a coordinate, nonhierarchical power relationship with teachers, we were able to encourage a more open and honest exploration of the issues presented. Second, "unhurried, systematic reflection" (Caplan, Caplan, & Erchul, 1993, p. 26) during the teacher's first year creates a unique opportunity to increase the teacher's awareness of possible solutions available to address her concerns. In fact, Schön (1987) believes that providing teachers with opportunities to formally and informally reflect on their practice is one of the most critical methods for helping teachers develop into thoughtful and effective practitioners. Furthermore, consultee-centered consultation groups appear to promote what Reiman, Bostick, Lassiter, and Cooper (1995) term "relaxed reflection," which they believe is critical for assisting novice teachers to "make meaning from their new complex roles" (p. 109).

Another critical feature of some consultation groups (e.g., Bergan & Kratochwill, 1990; Caplan & Caplan, 1993) is the importance placed on the problem-solving process. In this form of group consultation, it is essential that the facilitator engage in a dialogue that helps the teacher view the problem from multiple perspectives, reframe the problem if necessary, and generate hypotheses about the problem that will lead to possible strategies or solutions to address the concern. According to Zins (1993), "the consultation process may be facilitated through *overt cognitive modeling of the problem-solving process*," (p. 188) and consultants can explicitly emphasize the stages of the problem-solving process to help teachers better understand the goals of consultation. In our New Teacher Groups, we explicitly described the problem-solving process we followed to provide the participating teachers with a framework for thinking about the issues they were encountering in the classroom.

Use of Consultation in Our New Teacher Groups
The problem-solving process provided the teachers with a structure that served to focus and guide their discussions. This process also provided a framework for thinking about the issues encountered in the classroom, now and in the future. We therefore organized the group meetings around discussions that focused on current problems and concerns presented to the group by the teachers (Harris, 1995; Hollingsworth, 1992). Although the problem-solving process is just one aspect of the overall consultation model utilized, it was the only feature that we explicitly presented to the teachers in our New Teacher Groups. In the next section, we more fully describe how we implemented the problem-solving model by focusing on the issues and concerns of the group members.

Problem-Based Discussions
Participation in the New Teacher Groups encouraged the development of teachers' ability to reflect on issues critical to successful teaching through the use of problem-based discussions. *Problem-based discussions* are those in which each beginning teacher shares issues and concerns with the entire group; in turn, the group, under the guidance of the facilitator, works to help the teacher better understand and resolve the problem. The group facilitators used the following structure to guide the problem-solving discussions at the meetings:

- A teacher presents his or her problem to the group.

- The facilitators and the group work together to help the presenting teacher gain a clearer conception of the problem and generate alternative interpretations by asking questions and pushing for clarification and further refinement of the definition of the problem.

- Once the problem is defined, the group assists the presenting teacher by either discussing additional information needed to understand the problem or brainstorming possible solutions, and developing an initial plan of action.

• At subsequent meetings the teacher provides follow-up reports on the implementation of the plan, which allows for further exploration and collaborative assistance from the group members (see figure 1 for an illustration of the problem-solving process).

While the problem-solving process was at the core of our New Teacher Group meetings, we also developed a structured format or routine for conducting the groups. In the next section, we outline a typical agenda to paint a picture of how our groups were conducted.

A "Typical" Agenda for the New Teacher Group Meetings

The New Teacher Groups usually met in a teacher's classroom after school. Each session was held in a different teacher's classroom and the hosting teacher was responsible for providing refreshments as well as for conducting a brief tour of her or his classroom. The one-and a half-hour meetings included the following elements:

- **Each teacher in the group briefly shared** something that went well and/or something that did not go so well for them that week. (The teachers called this "brags and drags.") We found that this served as a good icebreaker by giving everyone the chance to talk at the beginning of each meeting. It provided teachers with a rare opportunity to focus on the positive aspects of their work and to receive some acknowledgment from the group for a job well done. This activity also gave the facilitators a sense of who needed additional time to discuss their issue during the meeting.

- **Follow-up reports from the teachers** whose problems were discussed at the last meeting were presented. The amount of time spent on follow-up reports varied quite a bit. Occasionally, it involved a quick update on a child or situation. In other cases, it became the focus of the group's problem-solving agenda.

- **Two or three teachers volunteered to share an issue, problem, or concern** that the group then helped to define more clearly and assisted the presenting teacher in creating a plan of action to address the problem. The presenting teacher's problem posed to the group might be new or it may be a follow-up of an issue previously discussed.

- **The group engaged in the problem-solving process** with two or three teachers. As outlined previously, after the teachers volunteered to share their problems, the group helped the presenting teacher by working through the problem-solving process in the following manner: (a) the teacher presented his or her problem, (b) the group helped the teacher further define or redefine the issue, (c) the group and the teacher brainstormed possible solutions based on the presenting teachers' new conception of the issue, and (d) the teacher and the group created a plan for addressing the problem and for evaluating the outcome. We should note that although this was the framework for the problem-solving process, the actual discussions in the groups were rarely so linear and clear-cut. Often, the group would spend the entire session on helping the teacher understand the problem better by examining it from multiple perspectives.

- **An evaluation of the meeting occurred at the end of the session** when the facilitators asked the group what they thought did and did not go well in that day's meeting. This information was especially helpful to the facilitators as they planned future meetings.

Although we attempted to use this structure to guide our New Teacher Group meetings, they did not always follow this exact format. As in effective classroom teaching, a facilitator must be able to adjust and adapt the structure of each particular session to meet the needs of the teachers at that time. We thus had meetings in which the entire session was devoted to assisting one teacher. There were other meetings in which very little problem solving occurred; the teachers instead spent the entire time sharing their positive and negative school experiences from the previous couple of weeks. There is a fine line between a gripe session and the opportunity for teachers to truly express their problems and to gain assistance from the group. At times, the problem-solving structure became too restrictive and so the facilitators adapted and refined it to meet the needs of their group at specific meetings. However, we found that this problem-solving format is a powerful and productive way to structure the group discussion and to provide everyone with a framework for thinking about the process.

Once we made the problem-solving structure explicit, it became clear to the teachers that there was a logic behind our questioning and probing and they became engaged in the process of helping each other to fully understand their issues and problems rather than simply offering advice.

All of the groups explicitly discussed the problem-solving model we used to guide the discussions during the group's first meeting.

Although this structure appeared to be helpful in encouraging meaningful dialogue among the new teachers, it could not have happened without the leadership of the facilitators in each group. The group facilitators played an integral part in encouraging thoughtful and rich problem-based discussions in the New Teacher Groups. These discussions in turn helped provide social, emotional, and pedagogical assistance to the beginning teachers who participated in the groups. In the next section, we discuss the role that the facilitators played in structuring and modeling the problem-solving process in the New Teacher Group meetings.

The Role of the Facilitator in the Problem-Solving Process
The facilitators of the New Teacher Groups were charged with creating a safe and trusting atmosphere in the group, explaining and modeling the problem-solving process, monitoring the group dynamics, and encouraging the presenting teachers to commit to a plan of action.

Although the process of developing a trusting group atmosphere continued throughout the school year, it was incumbent upon the group facilitators to set the stage for the group environment during the first few group meetings. In the facilitators' initial descriptions of the purpose of the New Teacher Groups to the participating teachers, they explained their nonevaluative, nonjudgmental role, which was essential in creating a group environment where teachers could talk about their difficulties and insecurities. In the initial meeting, the facilitators also discussed the importance of confidentiality within the group.

We found that the most difficult task for the facilitator was assisting the teachers to ask questions that encouraged the presenting teacher to clearly define his or her problem. This was difficult because early in the year the teachers are much more eager to offer advice rather than to ask questions to help others gain new insights and varying perspectives on their problems. All of the teachers in our groups wanted to help their colleagues solve their problems, but this aid often came in the form of suggestions as opposed to attempting to better understand the context and complexity of the problems presented. This situation is not unique to our groups. Corey and Corey (1997) suggest that early in the life of a group, members are likely to offer suggestions and advice. They go on to say, "This may seem like progress, for there is the appearance of group interaction, but too much advice giving bypasses the necessity for people to work through their problems and discover their own solutions" (p. 136). We found that with the guidance and modeling of the facilitators over the course of the year, teachers became better at listening, better at questioning, and overall more thoughtful about defining the problem before they began making suggestions.

The facilitators' roles included helping the presenting teacher commit to a plan of action, whether that plan was to find out more information about the problem or to implement a new intervention idea or strategy. Moving the teacher from the talking stage to this action stage was one of the biggest challenges for group facilitators. This entailed moving the group discussion beyond the level of a complaint or gripe session to one of problem solving that could eventually result in a change in behavior, attitude, or understanding of the issue or concern.

We found that the facilitators themselves also needed support and an opportunity to discuss the difficulties they were encountering in their New Teacher Groups. We met biweekly with the facilitators to help them problem-solve about the challenges they were facing with each of the groups. Although a portion of our meetings with the group facilitators focused on logistic or research issues, we tried to provide each of them with time to present areas of concern with regard to how their groups were functioning. We had some interesting and productive discussion with the facilitators about such topics as encouraging the teachers' commitment to the group, building trust in the group, responding to a breach of confidentiality, and addressing racial issues that arose in the group. In the next section, we provide an example to illustrate the fluid nature of the problem-solving process and the role of the facilitator in guiding the teacher in self-reflection.

An Example of the Problem-Solving Process

The following is an illustrative example of the problem-solving process that was implemented during the New Teacher Group sessions. After carefully reviewing our transcripts we chose this example because it clearly exemplifies the teacher's internal struggle with the issue. The presenting teacher in this example was especially articulate in describing how changing her style in the classroom impacted her as a person as well as a teacher. The application of a Caplanian approach to consultation is evident in this example in that the facilitator helps the teacher to better define her problem and the group helps her see the problem from other perspectives. It is important to remember that the goal of this type of professional development is not a quick fix to solve the problem, but rather a long-term change in the way the teacher thinks about the problem and how she can address it. In other words, the emphasis is on helping the teacher become "unstuck" in her thinking about the problem and improve her problem-solving skills in order to find her own solution.

The following participants engaged in the discussion: Janet, a combination fourth- and fifth-grade teacher in her second year of teaching; Victoria, a first-year fifth-grade teacher; and Annette, a combination third- and fourth-grade teacher in her first year. The example focuses on a teacher who had difficulty with classroom management, especially in the eyes of her school administrators. She was struggling with how to define herself as a teacher and with how to gain more control of her class in a way that was compatible with her beliefs about children and how they learn:

> *Janet*: I think maybe it has something to do with [the fact that] you have [to have] respect for yourself. I'm not respecting myself or my job enough to demand certain things [from the students] and get them.
> *Facilitator I*: Is it that you don't quite know who you are yet or you know who you are and you're just not able to do it?
> *Janet*: I feel that I can get what I want [from the students] but not really [in a way] that I like to do it. And that's hard; that's hard too. But I can really do it, but I'm not happy. . . . Well, it's so personal. It really hits your core. It's like, do I have to change who I am to do this job?

Janet initially described her problem as not respecting herself enough to demand respect from her students and wondered out loud if she needed to change her sense of herself as a teacher to maintain order in her classroom. With the help of the facilitator's questions, Janet explained that she knew how to get the students to behave in a manner acceptable to her administrators (by becoming a stricter disciplinarian), but that she was uncomfortable with that role and with interacting with the students in that way. According the literature on teacher development, Janet's initial focus on herself is typical of beginning teachers. Bullough (1991) noted that "novices needed to possess a clear self-image of themselves as teachers before growth could occur: without a clear self-image, blindly imitating a cooperating teacher did not cause a lasting acquisition of classroom skills" (p. 146). It is evident that this emphasis on self-discovery and self-exploration as a teacher is well suited to a consultee-centered consultation approach. In this approach the focus is on the teacher rather than on the children. In some other models of consultation the focus would be on trying to create a behavior management plan to control the children without the element of the self-reflection on the teacher's part.

Two months later, this teacher again addressed the topic of getting the children to respect her, only this time as it related to the more immediate problem of being observed by the principal for evaluation purposes:

> *Janet*: Last Monday, . . . well I knew I was going to get observed [by the principal]. The previous week I was supposed to get observed and he forgot. I had this quote "perfect lesson" and he forgot. So I knew that I had to be observed again. And he would come. And so it was going to be a math lesson. And so I kind of worked on it. And then I talked to my mentor, Susan, and she said, "Janet, he's really concerned about behavior, and he really needs to see the students behaving." She was turning the heat on things. "Things had better be really together. Don't have a lesson too long. Make sure it's really clear and to the point." But, instructionally I'm really good. . . .

Although Janet was concerned with her students' behavior in the classroom she did not seem to have ownership of the problem at this point. The fact that she describes it in her mentor's words indicates that she sees the problem as something that others are concerned about rather than something that she would like to work on. One of the tasks for the facilitators was to help Janet focus on one aspect of her issue to begin to recognize that she has control over the outcome. This again illustrates the importance of a consultee-centered model—it is *Janet* who needs to generate what part of the problem to focus on. If the facilitators were to decide what strategy she should use or what approach she should take, it would perpetuate Janet's lack of ownership of the problem.

> Janet: And so I realized in the process of making lesson plans, I go . . . way over on instructional stuff, and get really excited about integrating material and how to get the kids interested. I don't really think about . . . the classroom management question and the basic steps. . . .
> *Facilitator I:* Organization. Transition.
> *Janet:* And the transitions. And I know transitions are hard but I don't ever really grin and bear it. . . . What can I do to make it

easier? You know, besides counting. Whatever, "you have five
seconds to get to your seat."
Facilitator I: So how are you going to do it?

Once Janet identified the part of the problem that she could work on,
the facilitator asked her to generate strategies for addressing it, perhaps
prematurely. Further exploring Janet's current strategies for ensuring
smooth transitions may have led Janet to a more productive solution:

> *Janet*: Ah, well, I'm meeting with (my mentor) tomorrow to talk
> a little about it. I guess I could try to have my lesson plans written
> out a week ahead of time so I could give them (to my mentor).
> . . . I feel like that may be what I need to do.

At this point, the problem is still outside herself; that is, something
defined by others that needs to be solved by others. The facilitators and
the group members might have helped Janet to think about less external
strategies by continuing to ask clarifying questions.

During a subsequent meeting, Janet described how she was very firm
with the students about the need for good behavior during the principal's
observation of the class. Although her "threats" were successful in
controlling her students' behavior, she was uncomfortable with this
method for managing behavior and promoting learning:

> *Janet:* But I also felt a little fake when the children walked in
> extremely quietly and then sat down. You know, I wonder if the
> principal thought that I'd threatened them. . . . I mean, that's kind
> of what he's asking for.
> *Facilitator I:* It seems like what worked about that is you made it
> really, really clear to the kids what you expected.
> *Janet:* Right. Right.
> *Facilitator I:* And that's what paid off.
> *Janet:* Right.
> *Facilitator I:* And maybe it doesn't have to be the straight line
> walking to the classroom. But, you know, if you could translate
> that into your personality more and be really, really clear about
> that.
> *Janet:* Right, Right. Yeah, [the students and I] were trying to talk
> ahead of time more [about my expectations] and I think that helps.

Janet's interpretation of the experience was that by threatening the
students, she received a positive evaluation from her principal. She was

unhappy with this style of management, but holds the principal responsible, saying, "that's kind of what he's asking for." The facilitator attempted to suggest aspects of the successful strategy that Janet might be more comfortable using, to help Janet see the overall concept that clearly communicating expectations to her students might be beneficial. It is another teacher who summarized this view nicely:

> *Victoria*: But I do think that's what you're focusing on when you realized it in your lesson plans, "OK, I need to plan in how we are going to get from A to B without it turning to total chaos."
> *Janet:* Right. Right.
> *Victoria:* It sounds like that's not changing your personality or threatening. It's just that you need to maybe look at the structure of the transition of going from A to B a little bit more. And that will become your style.

It is worth examining the evolution of the problem definition in this example. The initial issue as presented by the teacher was a lack of respect for herself and confusion about her role as a teacher. Over the course of the discussion, she began to see the problem as something much more manageable and controllable. Janet's redefined problem was the need to actively plan the structure of her lessons as well as the content; that is, to be proactive in her classroom management approach. Both the facilitator and one of the group members played a role in the evolution of the problem definition by asking clarifying questions and suggesting strategies. As Janet struggled to identify her difficulty with classroom management, it also became clear that she was struggling with how to define herself as a teacher, similar to Bullough's (1991) finding that novice teachers first need a clear self-image. Until Janet could see that she had some control over the problem of management in the classroom, her attempts to resolve it were superficial and not likely to impact her teaching in the long run. This discussion is fairly representative of the types of discussions that occurred—the teachers were active in reflecting on their practice and engaging in self-exploration while supporting each other in this process.

In this illustration of the problem-solving process, several important elements of Caplan's model of consultation are present. First, it was necessary for the group environment to be a safe, nurturing place where teachers felt comfortable engaging in self-exploration. Second, it was necessary to devote sufficient time to the exploration of the issue in order to help Janet arrive at her own conclusions and to continue the discussion over several sessions. The process became one of the development of the teacher's understanding of herself in the role as teacher rather than simply the generation of a behavior management plan to quiet Janet's students. Third, the facilitators, as well as the other group members, had a structure in mind for moving the discussions past the point of simply describing the issue and empathizing. Based on our experience with the New Teacher Groups, it is clear that without a specific framework for engaging in discussion the teachers tended to immediately offer lots of specific strategies without first exploring the issue in depth, or were hesitant to assume that they could be of assistance and then stopped at the stage of empathizing with the presenting teacher.

We now turn to a description of the participants in our New Teacher Groups, a description of our data and our data collection procedures, and an overview of how we analyzed our qualitative data. Finally, we provide an overview of the types of issues discussed by the teachers in our groups. These issues ranged from concerns about individual children to difficulties working with other adults to frustrations with school politics.

Chapter 4

New Teacher Group Participants, Guiding Questions, and Research Methods

> **Loretta, a third-grade teacher**: This was our group and I liked that. I know you are doing a lot of research with this, but it didn't feel that way. It didn't feel like you had an agenda.

As stated by Loretta, although we were studying the process of providing group consultation support to beginning teachers, we tried to allow the groups to follow their natural course and refrained from promoting our "agenda." Our main concern was to provide teachers with a forum for professional dialogue and an opportunity to receive peer support. In the first part of this chapter, we describe our procedures for recruiting teachers to participate in our groups, present our research questions, and describe some demographic information about the teacher participants. We then provide an overview of our procedures for coding the qualitative data and our process for data analysis. In the last section we describe the types of issues that the teachers in our groups discussed.

New Teacher Group Study Procedures

Teacher Recruitment
Teachers were recruited for our study during the new teacher orientation meetings held by each school district at the beginning of the school year,

usually in August. We asked for about fifteen to thirty minutes of time during their meeting to describe our New Teacher Groups and our research study. In some instances we asked former group members to help us recruit teachers in their school system by attending this beginning-of-the-year meeting and describing their participation in the groups. We provided all beginning teachers with a handout that described the groups and the commitment required to participate (see Appendix A). We were able to offer the new teachers who participated in the groups credits toward renewing their teacher certification. Teachers who were interested in learning more about the groups were asked to sign a list with their name, phone number, and days of the week when they would be available to meet so we could contact them to organize the New Teacher Groups.

Facilitator Recruitment
During the first year of the study we conducted only one New Teacher Group and were able to facilitate the group ourselves. After this successful first year, we decided to seek grant funding to hire graduate students to facilitate several groups throughout the area. This allowed us to expand our project to additional school systems and to meet the growing demand for this type of induction year support. In the second and third years of the project we recruited graduate students in school psychology and teacher education programs to facilitate the groups. Each group was led by two cofacilitators from each program. Most of the school psychology students had taken a course on school consultation methods and were familiar with the consultee-centered consultation approach as noted earlier. All of the teacher education students were former teachers; they thus brought firsthand experience and a wealth of knowledge about the first year of teaching. We found that this combination of a school psychologist and a former teacher provided the novices with the opportunity to hear multiple perspectives on their issues and concerns. We provided a series of three two-hour training sessions for the group facilitators in which we reviewed our adaptation of the consultee-centered consultation approach. During this training the facilitators read a transcript of a group session from the previous year, participated in some role-play activities, and discussed the research procedures. The facilitators were also trained in the procedures for keeping extensive field notes on each of the group sessions. Field notes included attendance data and the facilitators' overall impressions of the group process. The format they were given for documenting the types of issues discussed included the following information:

- the name of the presenting teacher

- a description of the issue

- how the teacher framed the problem (i.e., teacher's problem, child's problem, and school's problem)

- how the teachers responded

- amount of time spent on the discussion

- any results of the discussion (i.e., teacher's plan of action)

The facilitators completed a summary sheet for each issue presented by the teachers at the group meetings (see Appendix B).

To organize the groups, we divided the teacher sign-up lists by geographic area and by the days of the week the teachers were available. A list of teachers was given to each pair of facilitators who were responsible for contacting the teachers and for scheduling the first meeting. During the first meeting, the research requirements were outlined, including the audiotaping of each session and the teachers' commitment to participate in an individual end-of-the-year interview. The teachers who agreed to participate signed an informed consent letter that outlined the research procedures. The facilitators also signed a consent form to acknowledge that their participation in the groups was also being examined as part of our research project (see Appendix C). The teachers who participated in our groups are described in the next section.

Participants in the New Teacher Groups
From 1995 to 1998 we conducted nine New Teacher Groups that met biweekly from October through May. A total of 49 teachers participated in these nine groups for the entire school year. An additional 6 teachers participated in some of the early group sessions, but did not complete the year, usually due to time constraints. Of the 49 teachers who were full participants, 48 were in their first year of teaching and one was in her second year. Forty (82%) of the teachers were women and 9 were men (18%); 44 (90%) were white and 5 (10%) were African-American. The overwhelming majority of the teachers were from middle-class backgrounds and in their early to midtwenties. However, 7 (15%) of the new teachers ranged in age from 30 to their late 50s. For these 7, teaching was their second career.

Almost 20% of the first-year teachers graduated from the elementary education program at the University of North Carolina at Chapel Hill. The remaining 80% of the teachers graduated from other teacher education programs in North Carolina and throughout the United States. They taught kindergarten through fifth grade in twenty-five different schools in five different school systems in the southern United States. These schools were urban, rural, and suburban and served children from a wide variety of ethnic, racial, and socioeconomic backgrounds.

Description of the New Teacher Groups

Our New Teacher Groups were composed of three to nine beginning elementary teachers with an average of five teachers per group. Groups typically met biweekly after school in a participating teacher's classroom for one and a half to two hours. On rare occasions, the groups met in someone's home or at a local restaurant. Groups usually met about twelve times over an eight- month period from October through May. All of the groups were audiotaped. The average attendance rate for each meeting ranged from 70% to 86% for all of the groups.

Guiding Questions

There were two broad questions that guided our research study. First, we wanted to examine what types of issues and concerns new teachers talked about in our New Teacher Groups. We were interested in this most basic level of analysis to determine if topics discussed in our New Teacher Groups were consistent with the literature describing the concerns of beginning teachers. Much of this literature is based on surveys or interviews with teachers at one point in time. Because our groups met over the course of the teachers' entire first year, we were interested in finding out what types of issues were discussed in this ongoing manner.

Our second guiding question focused on the teachers' perceptions of the groups; more specifically, what did the teachers see as the benefits of participating in a New Teacher Group? The individual end-of-the-year interviews were conducted by the facilitators and were the main source of data we used to answer this broad question. In the next section, we describe our coding procedures and analysis strategies.

Data Coding and Analysis

For this project, we used qualitative methods (Schatzman & Strauss, 1973) to analyze our data. Our data sources included the audiotape transcriptions of the group meetings (when available), the field notes written by the group facilitators, the transcriptions of the individual interviews with teachers, and the teachers' written responses to a questionnaire about the groups. For two of the nine groups, all twelve audiotapes of the sessions were transcribed. As a result of the limited funds, however, only selected sessions from the other seven groups were transcribed. All of the forty-nine individual interviews with teachers were audiotaped and transcribed.

Teachers' perceptions of the groups. The questions we asked teachers during the individual interview ranged from, "When did you decide to become a teacher?" to "Why did you show up for the group week after week?" to "What role did the group play in your teaching and in your life as a teacher?" (see Appendix D). In order to find out what it was about the groups that seemed helpful and not so helpful to the teachers, we read and reread the transcripts of the interviews, looking for patterns and themes in their responses, both within and among interviews. After carefully reading the transcripts several times we began to see concurrent issues and themes.

We each read all of the interview transcripts and took notes on the types of things teachers mentioned as being beneficial about the group. We started by writing descriptive codes next to sections of text that addressed this question. Codes have been defined as "tags or labels for assigning units of meaning to the descriptive or inferential information compiled during a study" (Miles & Huberman, 1994, p. 56). After examining our list of the ways in which teachers described their experience of participating in the groups, it became clear that there were two main categories of responses—the first being the benefits of the group and the second being the features of the group that supported problem-solving discussions. In the first category, we found that teachers were describing aspects of the groups that they found personally beneficial. For example, many teachers emphasized the importance of knowing that they were not the only ones experiencing fears and frustrations. Many also described the value of being listened to as well as the satisfaction they received from helping other new teachers. This first group of codes we called "benefits of the new teacher groups." After coding and recoding, three subcategories of benefits emerged from the data: (a) combating isolation, (b) helping teachers gain a better understanding of their teaching, and (c) preparing them to meet future challenges.

The second main category of responses described the features of the groups that supported dialogue and encouraged problem-solving among the teachers: (a) confidentiality, (b) agenda set by the teachers, (c) nonevaluative facilitators, and (d) the inclusion of only beginning teachers in the groups. First, however, we turn to a presentation of the types of issues and concerns that teachers discussed in the groups.

Types of issues discussed. To explore our first guiding question regarding the topics discussed by new teachers, we examined the transcriptions of the group sessions and the field notes. As suggested by Schatzman and Strauss (1973), the analysis of our qualitative data involved "discovering significant *classes* of things, persons, and events and the *properties* which characterize them" (p. 110). We conducted a content analysis (Agar, 1980) of both the fully transcribed group sessions and the field notes from the other groups. Initially, we examined the transcriptions and the field notes individually to determine the types of problems ("classes of things") that were discussed. After tentatively identifying eight types of problems, we each independently coded the transcriptions of the first three sessions. At this point, we discussed our codes and further refined their definitions. A problem was defined as an extended discussion of an issue (initiated by a beginning teacher) that was dialogic in nature. Furthermore, because several of the discussions involved complex issues, we allowed for problems to be coded in more than one category. For example, one discussion focused on a teacher's concern about meeting with a parent who was angry about how the teacher had handled a disciplinary matter in the classroom. The teacher discussed both how to address the child's needs as well as how to handle her interaction with the father; this discussion was therefore coded as both "working with parents" and "individual children."

We coded the remaining transcriptions and all the field notes independently and then discussed our findings until we reached a consensus. Next, the categories were examined to determine if there was any overlap. Consequently, the categories of working with parents, other teachers, and administrators were collapsed into a single category called "working with adults." The ultimate result was that six categories were identified from the session data.

Findings

Content of the Teachers' Discussions
One overall finding consistent with the teacher development literature (e.g., Harris, 1995; Kagan, 1992; Reiman, Bostick, Lassiter, & Cooper, 1995) was that, in general, the teachers were not asking for specific

curricular strategies and content, or ideas for particular lesson plans. Rather, the beginning teachers were exploring who they were as developing professionals and how they could best integrate all their content knowledge and expertise into the art of teaching and building relationships with children. Each of the content categories is described including some examples of the types of discussions that we coded in the category.

Individual children and their families. The most frequently discussed problem revolved around the special needs of individual children, which often included a discussion of their home and family lives as well. The teachers were concerned about how to handle children with special needs such as behavioral problems, learning disabilities, attention deficits, and accommodation plans. One group also discussed a child who was, in the words of one teacher, "just driving me nuts." Another student who generated much discussion and concern had a younger brother who died in a house fire during the school year. The group discussed with the teacher how she could help this child and his classmates as well as how to access additional mental health services in the school and the community. In general, the teachers seemed to feel that they had to address the special needs of these children on their own, with little outside support. Unfortunately, this was often true. The child whose brother died in the fire was not offered any mental health services at the school and the teacher was offered only limited assistance in discussing this tragedy with her class. One of the roles that the group played was to influence and empower the teachers to access services for themselves and for their students with special needs.

Working with other adults. The next most frequently discussed problem was working with other adults. This is a broad category that included issues in dealing with parents, teaching assistants, mentors, administrators, and other teachers. Communicating with parents was a common situation that the teachers struggled with, particularly at the beginning of the year. Several teachers discussed the challenge of dealing with difficult parents and how to best communicate sensitive information about their child—information ranging from a child who was stealing in the classroom to a child with autistic-like symptoms.

Another common issue was the teacher's relationship with her or his teaching assistant. This relationship was often strained because of the teachers' discomfort with supervising and evaluating an adult who was often much older than they were, who had more experience with children, and who may have had a very different philosophy of teaching. At this early stage in their career, the teachers seemed to have difficulty directing the behavior of another adult and assuming a position of authority.

It should be noted that most of the teachers in the groups were in their early to mid-twenties and starting their first careers. As young adults, they were also at the point of making many life-changing transitions (Zumwalt, 1982). Their first year of teaching was their first year as professionals and although they may have felt unsure of their expertise, they found themselves being viewed as the expert by parents, principals, and teaching assistants. Others were aware of the high expectations parents and administrators had of them and were afraid to admit that they needed help. Discussions in this category were often focused on providing the teacher with the knowledge, skill, self-confidence, and objectivity to interact more effectively with other adults.

Curricular and planning issues. The next most frequently discussed problems were grouped into a category we called "curricular and planning issues." Discussions in this category included how to plan lessons for the entire year, how to structure lessons and assignments to promote student independence, and how to plan activities for gifted children in the classroom. Although the teachers seemed to enjoy sharing creative ideas for some content areas, such as reading and math, the focus was less often on specific instructional methods. The teachers seemed to be concerned more with the "how" of teaching rather than the "what." That is, they more often discussed how to plan and manage time, how to assess students' progress, and how to prepare students for end-of-grade tests rather than focusing on specific curricular content. This is in line with Hollingsworth's (1989) finding that teachers need to have general managerial routines in place before they could focus on pedagogy and content knowledge.

Self as teacher. In this category, we grouped issues that dealt with the individual's development of his or her identity as a teacher and the associated stress of meeting the demands of the job. The discussions centered on the image of themselves as disciplinarians versus friends to the students, the need for relaxation and time away from school, and the need for validation of their efforts. If the curricular and planning issues can be described as the "how" of teaching, discussion in the self-as-teacher category can be seen as the "who" of teaching (Banner & Cannon, 1997). That is, the group members were discovering who they were as teachers, highlighting the importance of self-knowledge in becoming a teacher (Harris, 1995). It is important to note here that many of the discussions in other categories also contained elements of self-exploration and it could be argued that all of the discussions could be coded in this "self-as-teacher" category. For a discussion to be coded in this category, however, the teacher had to identify herself as the focus of the discussion. The emotional content of these discussions was generally high and the teachers seemed to appreciate the group setting as a safe place to work through these issues. The consultee-centered framework for the groups allowed for the discussion of identity development, while keeping the focus on work-related issues.

Politics in school and school climate. The next category that we identified focused on school-wide issues, such as the politics of the school. These problems included school climate and culture, lack of resources in the schools, end-of-grade testing, lack of collaboration among teachers, and difficulty accessing special services such as counseling and special education. New teachers' frustrations with the politics and policies in the schools, like the topics in the self-as-teacher category, led to several impassioned discussions in the groups.

Classroom climate and classroom management. The final category of problems that we identified from our group data included discussions about how to create an orderly yet positive working environment in their classrooms. Teachers talked about the need to gain the respect of their students, how to help the children "stop being nasty to each other," and how to best provide their students with positive feedback and support. The teachers talked about the use of class meetings as one strategy for helping children take responsibility for their actions. As in the example of the discipline style of Janet, a combination fourth- and fifth-grade teacher; most of these discussions were focused on helping the teacher become more effective with the entire class.

In summary, the problems that the teachers were interested in discussing were similar to what others have found in working with beginning teachers. Some categories, however, such as "working with other adults," have been largely overlooked in the literature. What is most surprising is that teachers are expected to address these complex, challenging issues on their own, with little outside assistance. Kagan (1992) asserts that preservice education programs (and one could argue induction experiences) need to "encourage novices to make their personal beliefs and images explicit, to study pupils, to compare ongoing experiences with preexisting images, to construct standardized routines, (and) to reconstruct the image of self as teacher " (p. 150). Traditional staff development models that focus on a series of content workshops often do not provide the opportunity for in-depth self-reflection and exploration necessary to support beginning teachers' professional growth. A consultee-centered consultation model, however, provides an arena for this type of professional development by focusing on the teacher.

Our analysis of the end-of-the year interviews with each teacher suggests that the New Teacher Groups seemed to be most beneficial in combating isolation and in creating a sense of community by providing frequent opportunities for beginning teachers to talk with, listen to, and help each other. We will also look more specifically at the characteristics of the groups that encouraged dialogue and that supported the problem-solving process.

Chapter 5

A Community of Learners

Pamela, a beginning fourth grade teacher: [I came to the group meetings week after week] just to be able to talk about issues. It was nice to talk with people who understood, who weren't so far removed from being a first-year teacher, who didn't make you feel stupid. . . . And it was very comfortable. I felt like it was a good exchange of ideas and other people's input. Everyone was very respectful of other people. . . it was just a great encouraging atmosphere. Sometimes when talking about problems you didn't find solutions—but by just verbalizing them, realizing you had support from other people and that other people were experiencing the same things; a lot of times you would identify the source of the problem. This was helpful because sometimes it's really very hard to identify why it is bothering you, or what is the bigger, larger problem.

As Pamela suggests, the groups have the potential to help beginning teachers deal with their classroom dilemmas while also addressing their loneliness and insecurities. By providing opportunities to engage in problem-solving discussions with other new teachers who are going through similar experiences in their schools and classrooms, the New Teacher Groups help beginning teachers develop a more complex and sophisticated understanding of teaching while also enhancing their knowledge of themselves as teachers (Babinski & Rogers, 1998). As discussed

43

previously, these teachers are especially vulnerable because of the unrealistic expectations placed upon them in their early years in the profession. Making matters worse is the hesitancy of most of these teachers to ask for help and the unwillingness (or the lack of opportunity) of others in their schools to provide assistance to them. The emphasis on autonomy and privacy that pervades the culture of most schools further exaggerates this problem (Britzman, 1986; Lieberman & Miller, 1984).

The comments from the New Teacher Group participants we interviewed at the end of each school year suggest that these first-year teachers believed the groups were beneficial in easing their psychological pain, combating isolation, and creating a sense of community. Later in this chapter we describe how the teachers perceived the impact of the groups on their personal and professional lives. First, however, we provide a framework for interpreting our findings by presenting other research on the experiences and needs of beginning teachers.

Combating Isolation and Creating Community

As noted earlier, the first year of teaching is both "dramatic and traumatic" for most beginners and "is marked by the harsh and rude reality of everyday classroom life" (Veenman, 1984, p. 143). Veenman believes that the first years are so arduous for new teachers that even the term *reality shock* does not adequately describe the difficulties they face each school day. "Reality shock" suggests something very brief, but according to Veenman, novice teachers actually encounter the assimilation of a complex reality which forces itself incessantly upon the beginning teacher; day in and day out" (p. 144).

Added to this prolonged and incessant shock of the first year is the fact that schools can be desolate and insulating places—places where it is difficult just to find someone to talk to about teaching, let alone get any real help from one's colleagues. New teachers struggle desperately as they attempt to grapple with the complexities and contradictions of teaching and their own personal and professional development within the individualistic culture of schools. Harris (1995) elaborates further on why the first year of teaching is so demanding and is also so crucial to one's development as a teacher:

> For any novice, assuming the responsibilities of a "real" teacher,
> while exciting, is an incredibly challenging experience, since in

addition to coping with the multiple demands of the job, she is simultaneously engaged in the process of constructing a new image or identity of herself as a teacher. And despite all her contact with others over the school day, she remains isolated from the very conversation and story sharing so important to this identity work. As she attempts to bring together, reconcile, and transform past and evolving understandings—about teachers and teaching, about learners and learning, about subject matter, and about herself, she must find a way to make sense of the bits and pieces of her life, her past experiences as a learner, her experiences in a particular teacher education program, and her experiences in the particular school context in which she works—and she must do so alone. (p. 21)

Given the sociocultural context of most schools, it is easy to understand why beginning teachers not only feel extremely lonely and isolated but are also afraid to reveal uncertainties about their practice. Lieberman and Miller (1984) explain that without genuine dialogue it is difficult for these teachers to feel supported and it is almost impossible for them to develop and grow professionally. They claim that without peer support and opportunities for peer interaction it is especially hard for first-year teachers to gain a "clear sense of the quality" of their own teaching. Lieberman and Miller insist that in order for beginning teachers to develop a deeper understanding of themselves as teachers, there must be a "safe place" for them to air their "uncertainties and to get the kind of feedback necessary to reduce the anxiety about being a good teacher, or at least an adequate one" (pp. 13-14).

The absence of this "safe space" and the chance for collaborative problem-solving dialogue among teachers contributes to feelings of isolation and hinders their ability to implement changes in their classrooms (Johnson & Pugach, 1996). As we just suggested, beginning teachers quickly become aware of this culture of teaching, in which autonomy and privacy are valued, and rapidly learn not to ask for help or advice (Britzman, 1986; Merseth, 1990).

According to the participating teachers, one of the primary benefits of the New Teacher Groups was that the groups helped alleviate some of the isolation they were experiencing in their schools. Almost two thirds of the teachers reported that the groups were a major source of social support for them. A few of the teachers even claimed that they would have quit their teaching jobs without the sustenance provided by the other members of their New Teacher Group. The group meetings offered them a unique occasion to engage in serious discussions about their work with others who were experiencing similar problems and challenges. New teachers were able to break through their isolation and to begin to deal with some of their confusion by the opportunity they had to talk, to listen and be listened to, and to help other beginning teachers in the group. We explain in more detail in the next section how talking, listening, and helping one another encouraged a sense of social and emotional well-being and worked to enhance the kind of collaboration that leads to community formation.

The Opportunity to Talk to Other New Teachers
One of the primary differences in the New Teacher Groups, compared to other meetings the teachers attended, was that they had the chance to really talk to other teachers about their work. As we have noted elsewhere, giving new teachers the opportunity to interact with their peers can be particularly valuable (Harris, 1995; Hollingsworth, 1992; Meyer, 1999; Reiman, Bostick, Lassiter, & Cooper, 1995). Participation in the groups allowed new teachers to meet regularly with other novice teachers who were going through similar experiences and facing many of the same challenges. Like Zins, Maher, Murphy, and Weiss (1988), we also found that teachers felt that meeting with others who were "in the same boat" or who were experiencing what they were experiencing, was one of the most meaningful aspects of the group.

As noted earlier, groups can provide a unique kind of support that teachers can not find anywhere else. Again, we want to reiterate Gottlieb's (1988) assertion that "As much as people need the emotional intimacy of a single confidante, they also need a sense of reliable alliance with a set of valued peers who are . . . sources of feedback regarding role perfor-mance in diverse life spheres" (p. 23). Lucille's comments, and the quotes from other new teachers that follow, illustrate Gottlieb's (1988) claim about the value of peer feedback and support. Lucille, a third-grade teacher, articulated the unique value of conversing with other new teachers in this way:

> It's one thing to talk to your mentor about things—and I love my mentor . . . she's wonderful—but [the other beginning teachers] can relate to you so much more because they are going through the same thing. Or, they have the same kind of things going on in their personal lives too. [It's important] to see other people my age who are successful and love teaching. It is helpful having people you can turn to who understand what you're going through.

Maria, a new first-grade teacher, said that the group gave her "support that could not come from anywhere else except people in the same boat as myself." Annette, a combination third- and fourth-grade teacher, also spoke of the importance of discussions with her peers:

> I really enjoyed hearing other people talk about concerns and issues I was also having, because . . . sometimes I feel like, all the other [veteran] teachers were saying, "Oh, it is your first year and it is really tough and yada, yada, yada." But they weren't in the same place as I was. And it is one thing to have experience and another *to be experiencing.*

It became apparent to us that these new teachers valued the opportunity to share their teaching experiences, good and bad, with other first-year colleagues they trusted and cared about, and who cared about them. The support and sense of community that arose from the group was echoed by Pamela, a fourth-grade teacher. She attested to the uniqueness of the New Teacher Groups when she said having "someone there who cares for you in your struggling," was something she couldn't get at school even though her colleagues at school were "very, very supportive." Pamela also emphasized that participating in a group with "people who were experiencing the same things was helpful."

The responses of these new teachers are consistent with others' findings (Gottlieb, 1988; Hollingsworth, 1992; Meyer, 1999; Reiman, Bostick, Lassiter, & Cooper, 1995) regarding the unique value of peers for the development of beginning teachers. Creating this kind of trusting community environment, where people can talk about any and all situations they experience, gives teachers a supportive and constructive place to deal with the frustrations of the job. According to many of the new teachers, the group meetings provided a space where they could "unload" their disappointments, concerns, and frustrations. For example, Eleanor, a second-grade teacher, claimed that the new teacher meetings were "an excellent place to vent and know it would stay in the group." Loretta, a third-grade teacher, also spoke of the significance of having a place where one could talk safely about the many frustrating issues teachers encounter far too often in their schools. Loretta, as well as some of the other new teachers, succinctly described this outpouring of frustration as "venting." She stated emphatically that one of the things she liked most about the group meetings was that "I could vent. Then I could go home and live."

The New Teacher Groups were the one place where the teachers felt comfortable discussing their problems and frustrations. Like Loretta, some of the other new teachers even went so far as to claim that participation in the group saved their relationships with friends, housemates, and family. Lisa, a K-3 special education teacher, explained that "talking [to the group] probably kept me from driving close friends insane." Like Lisa, Marlene, a first-year second-grade teacher, made comments that are typical of those made by other new teachers in the groups:

> I liked meeting with other people to hear about what was happening to them, and I also liked having the chance to vent, or even just talk about what was going on. [The group] was a good outlet because my friends and my boyfriend, who aren't teachers, were getting really tired of hearing about it. And it was good to talk with somebody who was going through the same thing that I was.

In fact, about one fifth of the teachers specifically mentioned the significance of having a venue in which to "vent" their concerns to others who would understand their frustrations. Corey and Corey (1997) describe venting or catharsis as therapeutic because of the release of energy that one feels after expressing pent-up emotions. After venting, however, it is important that group members "work through feelings that emerged, ... gain some understanding of the meaning of the experience, and also formulate new decisions based on their understanding" (p. 250). It is important that the teachers gain a cognitive framework for seeing their problems from new perspectives.

Thus, the opportunity to express one's overwhelming concerns through "venting" and the subsequent cognitive work that ensues is extremely important for beginning teachers. Perhaps just as importantly, however, these opportunities to talk give teachers the chance to tell their stories and express their concerns to knowledgeable and sympathetic listeners whom they respect and trust. It became very clear early in the project that although talking about their experiences was incredibly important to teachers, listening and being listened to was also immensely valuable to them.

The Importance of Listening and Being Listened To
As a result of the self-doubt and the isolation that they undergo in their first year, new teachers also desperately need a group of people they can trust. Trust is gained through the chance to talk to others who are willing to listen. Listening provides a means of affirming others while learning more about oneself; thus it is through listening that we create the space both to attend to others and attend to ourselves.

, Yet, despite our understanding of its worth, all too often we diminish or ignore the importance of listening. In order to enact the power of listening in our New Teacher Groups, we created what Brownell (1993) calls a "listening environment"—a place where listening is encouraged, valued, and supported. Brownell claims that healthy listening environments enhance the perception of colleagues as "supportive and trusting," which in turn "has implications for the way individuals view traditional boundaries between personal and professional lives" (p. 242). By creating collaborative conversation groups where a "listening attitude" encouraged honest and open dialogue (p. 256), we believed that we could genuinely assist new teachers in coping with the challenges of the first year, while simultaneously helping them gain a better understanding of themselves as teachers.

In addition to the promotion of a "listening attitude" as proposed by Brownell (1993), we also tried to encourage what Bruneau (1993) calls "empathetic listening" in our New Teacher Groups. He defines empathetic listening as respectful of the dignity of others . . . a caring, a love of the wisdom to be found in others whoever they are" (pp. 194-195). He believes that listening empathetically can have a powerful impact on relationships with others and also on the development of self-understanding. Listening continually encourages us to "see ourselves from other perspectives" by "discovering our own special uniqueness in others which, in turn, "helps us to unfold our own individuality" (p. 195).

Not only is it valuable to listen to others, but it is important to have others really listen to you. Tournier claims that "it is impossible to overemphasize the immense need humans have to be really listened to, to be taken seriously, to be understood" (as cited in Powell, 1969, p. 5). New teachers are expected to listen to administrators, parents, mentors, and other colleagues as they give them orders and "advice" about everything from teaching, children, and the state curriculum standards, to the policies and procedures of the school. Even if some of this advice is helpful, the issue here is that while new teachers are forced to listen" to others, no one at their school is ever really listening to them. Outside of school, new teachers may be fortunate enough to have friends, relatives, or acquaintances who take the time to really listen to them. However, these individuals usually do not have the teacher orientation and classroom experience needed to genuinely listen to teachers' problems, frustrations, or successes in a very useful manner. In short, beginning teachers are seldom afforded the support of a knowledgeable person who will seriously and sympathetically listen to them talk about teaching and their lives as teachers.

This need to be "really listened to, to be taken seriously, to be understood" is especially critical for beginning teachers who are struggling with issues of competence, respect, and identity. As Wardhaugh (1985) states, "the ability to appear adequate and normal is one of your most precious possessions, but one that you must also grant to others" (p. 12). Attentively listening to other new teachers and having them, in turn, listen carefully to you, provides a beginning teacher with a much-needed opportunity to be "taken seriously" and "to appear adequate and normal" at a time when she feels she is constantly being evaluated and everything in her life is in a continuous state of flux.

Having someone willing to really listen is particularly salient for new teachers in this tumultuous and difficult first year. Purdy (1997) contends that listening is central to developing and maintaining relationships with our friends and professional colleagues. This truly fundamental need to be listened to can be seen in the response of Rebecca, a third-grade teacher. As Rebecca said, she was overwhelmed, discouraged, and disappointed in her first year in the profession. However, Rebecca claimed that through the careful listening and thoughtful responses of the teachers in her New Teacher Group, she was able to get the social support she desperately needed from others in the teaching profession. She explained,

> I feel good about the fact that [the teachers in my New Teacher Group] were willing to listen and that they understood that I, and the other teachers at my school, were going through a hard time. And that they were able to sit there and listen to us and be very sympathetic and give us ideas and try to help us out. They were genuine and their apparent concern really helped me out. That is exactly what I needed.

The teachers found it valuable to listen to other beginning teachers talk about their difficulties during the first year, but, as Rebecca suggested, it was especially meaningful to have other teachers really listen to them. As Hillary, a beginning third-grade teacher, claimed, "It is always good to have someone who is ready to listen to you. . . . Like our New Teacher Group, we are ready to listen to each other [because] we're all going through it. . . . In the outside world, people aren't ready to listen."

Confirmation through Listening

· Providing new teachers with the opportunity to be listened to by other teachers who are "ready to listen," and who understand and appreciate their circumstances gives them the chance to be taken seriously, to be confirmed (Cissna & Anderson, 1994; Tournier as cited in Powell, 1969; Wardhaugh, 1985). Confirmation by one's trusted and respected peers is especially important at this time in the personal and professional lives of new teachers as they are constantly questioning their competence. Chandler, a K-3 foreign language teacher, explained that the group's attentive listening afforded him a sense of respect:

> I felt totally comfortable [talking about] any situation I had, whether good or bad, whether it was to brag to some people, or whether I needed to vent . . . I felt I would be respected and my problems were taken seriously and not blown off. I felt like as a first-year teacher I didn't get any of that [anywhere else].

All teachers, but especially beginning teachers, have an immense need to be confirmed. Cissna and Anderson (1994) claim that the need for confirmation is absolutely "essential to all of us for the emergence of a healthy self," and confirmation "is fundamental to any process we call dialogue" (p. 25). They posit that though confirmation is hard to define, it "involves the process through which people are 'endorsed' by others, ...[it] expresses awareness of the worth or significance of the other and accepts or endorses the validity of the other's experience" (pp. 23-24). Collaborative conversation groups are important because they can create multiple opportunities for confirmation to occur during teacher discussions. The chance to engage frequently in genuine dialogue is thus important for beginning teachers because it not only encourages the communication of ideas and emotions and the co-construction of new insights, but it is also a powerful vehicle for the confirmation of themselves and others.

As we considered creating support groups for new teachers we recognized the importance of providing the opportunity for teachers to express and receive the "endorsement" of their colleagues. What we did not want to do was design a forum where new teachers came together just so they could have a chance to "feel good about themselves" in a naive or uncritical manner. As Anderson, Cissna, and Arnett (1994) suggest, "Confirmation does not mean that one is simply treated nicely, or that one is always agreed with, or that anything one does is OK and that one is never corrected" (p. 71). Through dialogue we can endorse the validity of a teacher's experience without agreeing with her assessment of a given situation or the way she dealt with a problem. Again, the confirmation of another teacher does not necessarily mean that you agree with or sanction her ideas or actions. It simply means you recognize her worth as a person and the legitimacy of her claim to be a teacher. It seems that through talking and listening thoughtfully to one another in collaborative conversation groups, teachers are afforded the chance for confirmation. As a result, they begin to feel a lessened sense of social isolation.

Over and over again in the New Teacher Groups we witnessed the power of careful and sensitive listening. Another new first-grade teacher, Laura, also attested to the value of being listened to, "[It] is a good feeling when you can get that number of people together and feel like what you have to say is important—there was never a time that I felt like anyone disregarded anything." As illustrated by the comments from Laura, Chandler, Hillary, and Rebecca, the act of having someone really listen to you is critical for enhancing the social and emotional well being and professional development of beginning teachers. Listening conscientiously to others expresses a form of respect that new teachers seldom get anywhere else. Careful listening also gives the implicit message to the speaker that she is not only cared for, but that the listener views her as a competent individual who deserves to be taken seriously. In the next section we explore the role that helping others also plays in reducing one's sense of isolation.

Helping Others and Commitment to the Group
One of the findings from our interviews that surprised us was the value teachers placed on the opportunity to assist one another. In fact, almost one third of the new teachers claimed that one of the major reasons for their continued participation in the group was a result of the satisfaction they gained from helping each other. For example, Virginia, a beginning K-1 teacher who struggled desperately through her early weeks on the job, claimed that,

> Some people were going through worse things than I was and I felt like I could try and help. . . . I felt an obligation to be there because people were expecting me to be there. I thought that if they expected me to be there, then I could help them. That is what this group is [about], to rely on people that you trust to help you through the things that other people can't.

Like Virginia, Maria was another new teacher who had a difficult transition to the classroom early in her career. Maria was a new first-grade teacher from the Northeast. She was hired just five days before school started, and yet the school system expected her to move to a new state, find a place to live, and begin teaching on the first day of school. Despite the callous manner in which Maria was treated by her school district administrators, she, like Virginia, believed it was extremely important to do her best to assist the other new teachers in the group. Maria explained, "I felt like it was important to keep up with everybody and how they were doing. Even if I didn't have a particular problem, I felt it was important to be there for somebody who did."

Maria's and Virginia's strong desire to assist others in the group is similar to Hollingsworth's (1992) findings that relationship development is a critical factor in learning to teach. Hollingsworth claims that "the development of ongoing relationships and establishment of trust was important to the development of [teachers'] own voices and [their] learning about the issues" (p. 399). The teachers developed a strong bond with, and a sincere commitment to, their colleagues in the group. We, like Hollingsworth, found that the focus on relationships in the group seemed to encourage the teachers to become more patient with themselves and more tolerant of each other's perspective during group discussions.

Jeffrey was another beginning teacher who enjoyed helping the other teachers in his group. Jeffrey was an especially confident new first-grade teacher who initially was hesitant to join the group because he was unsure of how it might benefit him. Jeffrey enjoyed talking in groups. In fact, as an undergraduate he described himself as one of the most verbal teacher education students in his program. When he was asked at the end of the school year why he regularly attended the group meetings, Jeffrey said,

> It made me feel good because I was able to help people . . . at the beginning I probably did a lot more [talking] and then [I] settled into more of a listening role because everybody else was talking more. If I saw that somebody needed help, or needed some sort of backup, I could throw in a comment and make them feel like they weren't out in left field.

Chandler, the foreign language teacher from another group, summed up the feelings of many of the participating teachers when he stated simply, "I like to listen and I like to help." Like Chandler, Jeffrey, Maria, and Virginia, we found that most of the new teachers shared this desire to help their peers. This altruistic behavior on the part of these teachers seemed to promote their participation in the group and to create a sense of community. Helping others in the group appeared to simultaneously grow out of, and encourage, the development of relationships among the group members. It seemed these helping acts were accomplished out of a genuine sense of care and concern for the others in the group.

What occurred during the times when teachers helped each other can be characterized by what Noddings (1992) terms *engrossment* and *motivational displacement*. By engrossment Noddings means that in the act of assisting another there is an openness and sensitivity that is marked by attention and "full receptivity" (pp. 15, 16). She explains motivational displacement in the following manner: "Just as we consider, plan, and reflect on our own projects, we now think what we can do to help another" (p. 16). The words expressed by the teachers about their colleagues in the New Teacher Groups seemed to exhibit the kind of genuine caring described by Nodding's explanations of engrossment and motivational displacement. In fact, caring relationships between many of the members in the group were spawned by their participation in a New Teacher Group. These relationships helped the teachers feel respected, necessary, and welcomed by their colleagues in the groups and worked to combat their feelings of powerlessness and isolation.

While important in its own right for construction of community and caring relationships between teachers, helping colleagues also disrupts the pervasive role of privacy in schools that forms the foundation for the "culture of teachers" (Britzman, 1986), as noted earlier. By listening carefully and helping each other as part of the problem-solving process, many of these teachers learned how to collaborate and gained new respect for their peers in the teaching profession. We believe that this collaborative problem-solving activity, steeped in caring relationships formed in the New Teacher Groups, makes it possible for new teachers to build similar relationships and to provide similar forms of cooperative assistance to their colleagues in their respective schools.

Despite its potential for encouraging confirmation and the building of community, dialogue also offers the potential for debate and criticism. Those engaged in genuine dialogue are not simply telling one another exactly what they want to hear. According to Cissna and Anderson (1994), "contrary to some popular conceptions, dialogue does not preclude heated or even agonistic exchange. It does, however, presume sincere caring about the future of the other, the relationship, and the joint project of sense-making, rather than a primary focus on just winning or losing" (p. 14). Furthermore, they assert that collaborative learning communities, built on the opportunity to openly and honestly talk about one's lived experiences, can become "powerful sites" for "collective as well as individual growth and development" as a result of the support and critique that one receives from others through dialogue (p. 9).

Participating in dialogue by sharing teacher narratives and other forms of conversation encourages the creation of a community of learners while concomitantly enhancing the development of a deeper sense of oneself as a teacher. In fact, P.G. Friedman (1993) claims that "narratives play an important role in small groups by sustaining members' identity and interactions with each other and outsiders" (p. 207). We believe that discussion groups are essential because they provide new teachers with the chance to feel part of a group and part of the profession by engaging in serious conversations with others like themselves.

We began this section citing isolation and lack of community as some of the greatest difficulties that new teachers face in their early years in the profession. As we have seen, when our New Teacher Groups provided the opportunity for teachers to talk, to listen and be listened to, and to help each other through problem-solving discussions, some of the anguish of isolation was relieved. In their function as a forum where teachers learned to talk and work with each other, the groups encouraged the development of a community of learners. Furthermore, the New Teacher Groups provided a space for beginning teachers to "talk and be heard as they figure out who they are and what they know" (Richert, 1992, p. 194). We will now further explore this notion of beginning teachers examining who they are and gaining a better understanding of themselves as teachers by engaging in collaborative conversations with their peers.

Chapter 6

Gaining a Better Understanding of Oneself as a Teacher and Preparing for the Future

> **Craig, a fifth-grade teacher**: I think having some sort of setting where you are in a sense constantly saying "this is the way I am as a teacher" [made an impact on me.] Whenever you have to verbalize something it puts a whole new perspective on it. So by having a situation like [our group where you could] verbalize what you are doing and think out [loud] what you could have done differently and what you are going to do next time, it was a way to mold us as teachers.

We, like Harris (1995), believe that teachers are "made not born." They are continuously learning about their work and themselves and are therefore constantly developing and redefining who they are as teachers. As noted earlier, the first years of teaching are an especially critical time for the development of a personal and professional sense of self (Feiman-Nemser, 1983; Grant & Zeichner, 1981; Harris, 1995). As novices with little classroom experience and only a developing expertise, new teachers have a limited awareness of the multiple professional roles expected of them. Typically, student teaching practica focus almost entirely on instructional and managerial roles in the classroom. Few new teachers have many opportunities in their preservice teacher education programs to act and respond to various individuals such as parents, other teachers, administrators, specialists, and social workers, or to situations such as parent conferences, referring a child for special services, or testifying in court on a child's behalf. Opportunities for new teachers to engage in dialogue with their peers about these multiple roles can assist them in gaining a better understanding of themselves as teachers.

Gaining a Better Understanding of Oneself as a Teacher

In addition to helping new teachers deal with the loneliness and social and emotional problems they encounter in their first year as noted earlier, Harris (1995), like us, believes that it is imperative that we "find ways to support [new teachers] as they begin to develop their professional identities, so that they are able to become more like the kind of teachers they envision themselves to be" (p. 5). It is this process of support that "ultimately shapes the visions that guide their practices and defines their sense of 'self-as-teacher'" (p. 5). Banner and Cannon (1997) also suggest that what is missing from teacher education courses, in-service programs, and even conversations among teachers themselves, is a consideration of the human qualities of the people who teach. They contend that "[s]elf-knowledge is the missing dimension in our preparation and growth as teachers" and that we emphasize the "what" and the "how" of teaching and neglect the "who" (p. 42). Banner and Cannon insist that by ignoring the "who," we hurt not only our teachers, especially our novices, but our students as well.

Providing new teachers with opportunities to talk about teaching is critical to enhancing their professional growth and listening to their peers talk about their experiences in schools may be equally valuable. While we have previously described the importance of listening and storytelling to encourage self-reflection, listening is also salient to the process of gaining a voice—in short, fostering a sense of *identity as a teacher*. Coles (1989) claims that when we listen to someone else's story we can share their lives by experiencing their joys, their pain, and their perceptions—almost as if we were seeing it through their eyes. By talking together, teachers can overcome the limits of bounded rationality and become better able to process the infinite complexity of teaching and learning to teach. Part of this process involves listening to the ideas of their colleagues and comparing those ideas with their own (Richert, 1992).

Thinking Out Loud: The Problem-Solving Process
Through teachers' participation in the New Teacher Groups in general, and in the problem-solving process in particular, they were encouraged to

more clearly define themselves as teachers. As Schwab (1976) notes, educators learn more about themselves "through involvement with others—involvement in problems, involvement with elements of the culture" (p. 5). The problem-solving process in our groups prompted teachers to reflect and learn more about their teaching and themselves as teachers by allowing them to talk about their issues with their peers for extended periods of time. This problem-solving process permitted new teachers to "think out loud" and publicly reflect on their teaching by presenting their problems to the group. It also encouraged those who were not presenting to really listen and contribute to the discussion by asking sensitive and responsive questions. Such careful listening and thoughtful questioning invited participants to analyze their own teaching as well as their colleagues' practices.

Craig, a fifth-grade teacher, claimed that he and the other teachers acquired new insights into their teaching and greater knowledge of themselves as teachers because they felt like they were *invited to talk* about their problems in the group. Craig asserted that talking about an issue helps to put it into perspective. Marilyn, a K-1 special education teacher, also felt that she was more reflective about her teaching as a result of her participation in the group. She said, "[I became] a little more self-aware and also more willing to probe my thoughts and feelings about what was going on in school and what was going on with my kids in the classroom . . . it helped me clarify my own thoughts." Victoria, another fifth-grade teacher, described how the problem-solving process helped her think about how to deal with the day-to-day issues she confronted in her classroom:

> If I am having a specific problem with a specific child . . . it is very hard to step away from it and look at it objectively. The group is really good at saying, "OK, have you thought about this?" Or asking questions you haven't asked yourself . . . maybe things you haven't taken time to think through yourself . . . [and] that gets you thinking more about the problem. We all have different philosophies of teaching. . . . [So you get] suggestions and ideas from people who teach differently and who do things differently. It is always helpful. I might think [to myself], "No, it doesn't really sound like me." [But then] I might think, "Well, that part of it is good and I can take it and adapt it to what I want it to be."

As Victoria explained, the opportunity to hear the other teachers' perspectives is a critical piece of learning to teach. The teachers who were just quoted illustrate that the New Teacher Groups provided novices with a chance to understand themselves as teachers by offering them a forum for discussing their experiences in schools. Richert (1992) explains the importance of teachers getting the chance to seriously discuss teaching with each other:

> As teachers talk about their work and "name" their experiences, they learn about what they know and what they believe. They also learn what they do not know. Such knowledge empowers the individual by providing a source for action that is generated from within rather than imposed from without. In Dewey's (1933) terms, teachers who know in this way can act with intent; they are empowered to draw from the center of their own knowing and act as critics and creators of their world rather than solely respondents to it, or worse, victims of it. (pp. 196, 197)

Jointly participating in problem-solving discussions is crucial to developing a sense of oneself as a teacher. Novices learn much about teaching, and about themselves as teachers, by engaging in collaborative conversations focusing on their practices (Hollingsworth, 1992). The stories that teachers tell each other about their teaching experiences provide them with a "sense of coherence" about their work (Friedman, 1993, p. 201). It is the *process* that is important, rather than simply hearing about how to address a problem. According to Corey and Corey (1997), "people learn more from hearing how others are engaged in a struggle than from hearing their solutions to their problems" (p. 144).

The beginning teachers in our groups felt that they were able to talk, listen to others, and reflect on their own teaching by engaging in the problem-solving process. The problem-solving process became a mechanism for structuring the conversation so that it became more than just a chance to gripe. This process allowed the teachers to use dialogue as a medium in which they could reflect on their teaching and broaden their understanding of the teaching profession. Another beginning teacher, Amanda, who taught second grade, described her experience in the group as "an escape from everyday activity . . . a time for me to sit and reflect on what had happened." She continued her comments by talking about the value of being "forced" to reflect on her practice—"sometimes all these things that may be bothering you, you may not actually have the chance to think through. But if you are forced to, then you can talk about them and think through them."

By talking and listening to others talk about a variety of issues relevant to their practice, these new teachers were able think more deeply about themselves in their roles as teachers. According to another group member, Christy, a second-grade teacher working in an urban school, the group problem-solving discussions, "made me analyze how I was teaching and what things were important to me. . . .It just opened my mind . . . and made me question some things." The comments of Amanda, Christy, Victoria, Craig, and others suggest that the group problem-solving discussions encouraged the new teachers to look more carefully at their practice and promoted the continued development of their understanding of themselves as teachers.

Developing a Voice

As noted earlier the act of teachers helping other teachers in the group appears to represent an example of genuine caring and concern (Noddings, 1992). Because occasions to help peers increased the chances for new teachers to confer authority on their own personal experience, this helping component promoted participants' acquisition of a better understanding of themselves as teachers. For example, Darren, a K-5 physical education teacher, reported that when he was able to assist other teachers by drawing on his expertise and practical knowledge, "It felt good to talk about a situation and know that someone else in the group benefited from my experience. Although I was a new teacher I had things I could give to my colleagues and that felt good."

The opportunity to share one's expertise may serve to promote teachers' greater knowledge of themselves in their role as teacher and to encourage their continued professional development because "Voice can be seen as the connection between *experience* and authority . . . [thus] giving authority to one's personal experience while learning to teach is *central* to understanding how and what one is learning from the experience" (Featherstone, Munby, & Russell, 1997, p. 3). It seems that drawing on experience in order to help colleagues has the potential for establishing one's authority and thus for strengthening or refining one's voice as a teacher. The seemingly straightforward acts of listening and thoughtfully responding to others' explanations of problems assist new teachers in helping one another gain a more vivid understanding of the issues they are grappling with while also developing their voices as teachers (Munby & Russell, 1994).

Furthermore, as Harris (1995) suggests, "Without interaction with others, we would not be able to reflect upon, learn from, or even recognize our experiences" (p. 10). Loretta, a third-grade teacher, described how her interactions with other new teachers assisted her in developing a more in-depth understanding of her own teaching. She claimed that the group discussions "made me think more about what I was doing, why I was doing it, and what am I going to do about it to make it better." Again, it was Craig, a fifth-grade teacher, who explained that by participating in the group he was able to reflect on his teaching and thereby further develop as a teacher in ways he could not do in other professional situations:

> I felt like we were discussing things I never got a chance to discuss at school. I couldn't have really discussed them in college because I didn't have the experience to draw upon. I enjoy hearing what other people are doing. It helps me think about what I am doing if I can hear what other people are doing. It helps me define myself a little more as a teacher if I know this is the way I am.

The New Teacher Group meetings provided novices with a forum to better define themselves as teachers because the groups offered them the chance to "teach" in a venue beyond their own classrooms. These meetings afforded new teachers the rare opportunity to use their own pedagogical knowledge to assist other teachers. In the process of helping their peers they were able to assert their authority and develop their voices as teachers by sharing their expertise with respected colleagues.

Gaining a Broader Understanding of the Teaching Profession
Part of acquiring a clearer understanding of "who I am" as a teacher is gaining a deeper awareness of the many different experiences and circumstances faced by other practicing teachers. By hearing specific details about what their peers experience in their work at different grade levels, in different schools, and in various teaching roles, new teachers in the group were able to broaden their perspectives of what it means to be a teacher and a member of the teaching profession. Teachers learned about differences in the micropolitics and policies of various schools and school districts. They talked about the different educational philosophies and leadership styles of principals and mentors. For example, Mark, a first-grade teacher, claimed that listening to other new teachers talk about their administration and their classrooms was extremely helpful because it gave him the chance to "look at something outside my classroom and outside my school." He felt it provided him with new perspectives on his teaching and new insights into the teaching profession.

Many of the new teachers were unaware of what some of their

colleagues did every day in their roles as teachers. For example, Marlene, who taught second grade, commented that she "knew nothing" about what special education teachers did and that she "learned a lot" about their job because of the discussions with the two special educators in her group. Paul, a rural first-grade teacher, also had a limited understanding of the role of the special educator in his elementary school until he listened to, and asked questions of, the special education teacher in his group. Even the fourth- and fifth-grade teachers in the groups had little conception of what the work lives of the kindergarten and first-grade teachers were like and vice versa.

Overall, it seems that providing new teachers with opportunities to engage in serious discussions about teaching with individuals who teach in a variety of different situations makes it possible for them to acquire a broader understanding of the teaching profession, which, in turn, helps them to more clearly define their role as teachers and as professionals. Meyer (1999) claims that the new teachers in the collaborative conversation group he co-facilitated "gained a *wider purview* of the profession" because the group was composed of beginning teachers from a variety of schools and teaching situations. He believes that the group's discussions "enabled the teachers to learn about school contexts, . . . collegial relationships, and perhaps most importantly, how and under what conditions students learn" (p. 227).

In sum, the New Teacher Group meetings appeared to afford beginning teachers with the opportunity to receive much-needed social, emotional, and psychological support while also enriching their understanding of themselves in their new roles as teachers as well as broadening their knowledge of the teaching profession. The groups promoted professional growth by offering teachers the occasion to increase their authority and to learn from one another by sharing their personal experiences and by drawing from their own expertise as teachers. In the following section we explain how the group discussions helped prepare new teachers for the weeks, months, and years to come.

Preparing for the Future

The responses of the teachers in the end-of-the-year interviews suggest that the New Teacher Group meetings offered them a means to ease some of their immediate frustrations and functioned as a remedy for the effects of their current isolation. These meetings, however, also served as a vehicle to renew the teachers' self-confidence and to help prepare them to meet the challenges they will face in the near and distant future. By sharing teaching strategies, curriculum ideas, and classroom stories, the group members exchanged information that they could adapt to their own teaching style and experiment with in their own classrooms. New teachers are often desperate for pedagogical ideas and many of the group discussions revolved around teaching strategies. Unlike the stereotypical teacher talk found in the traditional "make-it, take-it" workshops, the conversations that took place around teaching practices and classroom activities went well beyond simply sharing "cute ideas," "fun activities," or exchanging prepackaged sets of lesson plans. Teachers questioned one another about the value of their lessons, all the while critically analyzing their worth for their own students in their own classrooms. In addition, this process of listening and responding to their peers appeared to do much more than just serve as a medium for teachers to exchange and critique teaching ideas—it also prompted a renewed sense of hope and agency for these new teachers. We will now explain how the teachers perceived this process as beneficial to them.

Providing Encouragement and Inspiration
Many group conversations and problem-solving discussions offered the new teachers encouragement and inspiration. Words like *uplifting, inspiring* and *encouraging* were used by teachers to describe their experiences in the New Teacher Groups. Eleanor, a second grade teacher, felt that "just listening" to other new teachers talk about what they were doing inspired her to "work even harder." Another new teacher, Rob, a fourth-grade teacher, stated in the end-of-year interview that the group discussions provided him with the necessary feedback and support to help him "keep going" in difficult times. Rob maintained,

> When I have been working with a kid and exhausted all the different ideas I had about working with him. . . it was good to hear some feedback, to get some other ideas, because it made me think a little more. It made me think that hey, maybe it isn't over. I'm not defeated, there are other things, other avenues. Sometimes it gets so exasperating . . . [but] when you are with [the group], and you have people kind of plugging you on and saying, "Maybe you should try this" or "Have you tried this?" . . . It helps give you a little more energy to put into whatever problem it is.

In fact, Gottlieb (1988) claims that groups of peers can provide encouragement and support because their common experiences heighten their credibility and make them trusted sources of feedback and advice. Like Rob, Chandler, a K-3 foreign language teacher, felt both supported and motivated by the group. He noted,

> [T]he impact the group had was to instill in me a feeling of don't give up or don't let somebody close the door on you. And not to be afraid to open up even more. . . . By seeing the different situations that people have dealt with successfully it shows that anything is possible, but you can't settle for second best. And not to let the stigma of being a first-year teacher get to you.

These comments by Rob and Chandler corroborate Gottlieb's claim about the reinvigorating nature of peer support. Furthermore, Corey and Corey (1997) suggest that hope—"the belief that change is possible" (p. 247)— is an important therapeutic factor in group work. In a group setting teachers can encounter others who have struggled with similar issues and were able to successfully regain control over their situations.

The New Teacher Groups were particularly meaningful for beginning teachers because it is easy to become disheartened and discouraged during the early years in the profession. Many of the teachers who participated in the groups claimed that as a result of attending the meetings they felt more empowered to deal with the challenges they faced at school. As noted earlier, in addition to providing new teachers with encouragement, inspiration, and support to go back into their classrooms with a new sense of confidence, the group meetings were also places where teachers shared specific ideas about teaching.

Exchanging Teaching Strategies and Ideas
By hearing the classroom stories of other group members, the teachers acquired new strategies and practical ideas that they could draw upon the following day, the next week, or the next year. For example, Amy, a second-grade teacher, described what she learned from the other new teachers in her group:

> I really appreciated different ways of dealing with things. There was a music teacher who went from classroom to classroom so he had quick management ideas. We had a special education teacher in the group, which was helpful because I mainstreamed a couple of autistic children and she gave me ideas . . . in my teacher education [program] the exceptional child [course] . . . was so brief, it was just an overview.

The majority of the teachers described how the group shared specific teaching strategies, new approaches for discipline and classroom management, different ways of working with teaching assistants, and useful methods for communicating with parents. They also exchanged novel curricular ideas that they incorporated into their own teaching. Another teacher, Rachel, who taught fourth grade in a rural school, believed that the group "impacted her teaching for the better" because she had the opportunity to learn from others by "pick[ing] up on their strengths" and "then taking strategies back to her classroom." After hearing one of the other teachers talk in the group about her own classroom, another new third grade teacher, Naomi, incorporated more child-centered activities into her curriculum and adapted her teaching style to become more responsive to the children. Victoria, a fifth-grade teacher, explained how the group discussions that focused on teaching strategies encouraged her to reflect upon and more critically analyze her own teaching to adapt and refine her teaching repertoire:

> I tried things that I wouldn't have tried before because it never occurred to me to take that particular approach. . . . It was fun to see other people's rooms and get ideas. I think because we are such different teachers, it was nice to exchange that. It made me think more about what I was doing, particularly as I was starting to try to decide how I wanted to discipline and how could I do it differently. I thought about Hillary [a fellow new third-grade teacher] a lot. How would Hillary handle this same kid? Probably very differently from the way I just handled it. I think that was good.

It is clear that through these conversations, the teachers gained valuable insights and strategies that they were able to put into practice as soon as the next day, while other discussions that revolved around less common situations assisted teachers in thinking about how they might handle these challenges in the future.

Preparing for Unusual Future Situations

Listening and responding to the experiences of their colleagues gave the New Teacher Group members the chance to relive, reconsider, and reflect upon a variety of significant but rare classroom situations. These discussions granted the teachers a chance to talk, listen, and think about infrequent or extreme situations like the death of a student's parent, a child who was physically abused, an overly belligerent parent, or a student who brought a knife to school. Since situations such as these need to be handled thoughtfully and sensitively, it was beneficial for all teachers to have the chance to carefully consider ahead of time how they might respond.

These discussions were unlike a college lecture or workshop focusing on such topics like, "What do you do when a child brings a weapon to school?" or " How do you respond to a death in a child's family?" These problems were very real because they actually happened to a member of the group. Again we hear from Annette, a third- and fourth-grade combination teacher, who explained how certain discussions helped prepare her to deal with similar events that might occur in her classroom in the future:

> I learned a lot from hearing [Hillary] talk about her [student] who suffered from [the death of his brother] in the fire. It is very possible that could happen to someone I am working with. So I feel a little more prepared for those types of things.

The opportunity to talk and think about these extenuating but significant events is a valuable experience. Likewise, exchanging teaching strategies and receiving encouragement from other beginning teachers helped ease the isolation for many of these teachers while also enhancing their teaching repertoire.

Summary

The results of the interviews we conducted at the end of each year suggest that the teachers believed the groups were beneficial in (a) assisting them in acquiring a better understanding of the teaching profession, of their own teaching, and of themselves as teachers; and (b) preparing them to meet the challenges that they would face as teachers over the next weeks, months, and years.

New teachers clearly need the opportunity to talk with others who are going through similar experiences (Gottlieb, 1988; Harris, 1995; Hollingsworth, 1992; Meyer, 1999; Reiman et al; 1995; Zins et al; 1988). They also desperately need to be attentively and responsively listened to by knowledgeable peers (Bruneau, 1993; Friedman, 1993; Richert, 1992; Wardhaugh, 1985). The teachers in our groups also perceived the chance to get help from, and give help to, their colleagues as extremely important to their personal and professional well-being and to their development as teachers.

Collaborative conversations that center around problems invite teachers to think more about their work and about their personal and professional selves (Hollingsworth, 1992; Meyer, 1999). By talking and listening to other teachers converse about classroom problems and issues, the new teachers appeared to obtain both a broader understanding of their profession and new insights into themselves as teachers. Finally, the groups provided inspiration and encouragement that these beginning teachers could not find anywhere else. This group support gave additional strength and determination to the teachers so that they could persist and continue to do their best under difficult circumstances. It is clear that beginning teachers need a chance to talk to each other in a safe and supportive environment if they are to flourish in the teaching profession. The New Teacher Groups provide one promising way that this might happen. We will now examine the structural features and characteristics of the groups that made it possible to provide teachers with the support necessary to help relieve their stress while also enhancing their professional development.

Chapter 7

Group Features that Encourage Dialogue and Enhance Problem-Solving

> **Rhonda, a first-grade teacher**: [In the group] there were different conversations than I was having anywhere else because of the nature of the people involved and the way that we were able to discuss things.

The unique role of the New Teacher Groups was summed up well by Rhonda. The groups provided a setting which, unlike other situations, allowed teachers to talk freely and honestly about their work with others in their profession. This is a point that can not be overemphasized—there are few, if any, opportunities for novice teachers (let alone experienced teachers) to engage in extended discussions about teaching and about themselves as teachers.

As discussed throughout this book, the process of learning to teach requires that beginners have the opportunity to share their stories and to hear the personal narratives of their colleagues if they are to genuinely learn how to question, adapt, and refine their pedagogical ideas and practices (Harris, 1995; Hollingsworth, 1992; Meyer, 1999). New teachers need the chance to talk to each other so they can gain a better understanding of their personal and professional selves and to learn to work with one another as colleagues (Harris, 1995; Hollingsworth, 1992; Meyer, 1999). Rhonda went on to explain that "it's real difficult to have those kind of conversations here (in school). It's harder to put aside the time to have them within the context of the daily grind. Even when you set aside the time, it doesn't happen." As she suggested, the New Teacher Groups afforded an opportunity for "different" kinds of discussions than were happening in her school. Rhonda and many of the other participating teachers genuinely felt that without the New Teacher Groups they would have engaged in little, if any, serious dialogue about their work.

The structure of the groups encouraged relationships to develop whereby teachers would assist each other in a manner that other professional development experiences did not. For example, Mary was a friendly and likable nontraditional new third-grade teacher. At almost fifty years old, she had worked several "high-skill "jobs before tiring of the "profit hungry" private sector and entering the teaching profession. Mary began the school year feeling "very confident." This confidence was short-lived, however. She felt that "all of a sudden" she didn't "know what the hell" she was doing. Mary later said she felt like she got more support at her first job working at a dry cleaner than she received from her school as a beginning teacher. She claimed that she "didn't know what she would have done" without the support of the other teachers in the group. We believe that there are structural components of the New Teacher Groups that encouraged dialogue, reflection, and the development of trust and support that made it possible to help teachers like Mary.

Important Group Features and Characteristics

We have learned from our research and from our experience working with the New Teacher Groups that there were several critical structural features that appeared to enhance problem-solving, encourage dialogue and reflection, and provide support for beginning teachers in the groups.

Four Essential Features
Commitment to Confidentiality. Our most sacred guideline was that the group participants must maintain confidentiality at all times. Nothing discussed at the meetings was to be mentioned outside of the group. As Donna, a fourth grade teacher, explained, the group was "a place I could go and say what was on my mind. I could say how I felt about my school, my mentor, whoever, and know that it wasn't going anywhere." This guideline of strict confidentiality allowed the new teachers to talk about issues that they could not discuss anywhere else without worry-

ing about personal or political repercussions.

A critical by-product of maintaining confidentially was the development of trust among the participants. The explicit conversations about the importance of confidentiality provided the teachers with a sense of security that encouraged the formation of trusting relationships. A phrase used by many of the new teachers to describe the groups was that it was "a safe place to talk." Another teacher, Virginia, a K-1 teacher, spoke about her willingness to divulge sensitive information because of her trust in the group. She explained that the teachers in the group "weren't going to go around and tell [what they heard in the meeting]. So I trusted them with everything that I said." In fact, the promise of confidentiality itself was a critical factor in helping the teachers learn to trust one another to the point where they were able to discuss even highly personal and sensitive issues that exposed their innermost concerns and vulnerabilities. As stated by Corey and Corey (1997), confidentiality is "one of the keystone conditions for effective group work" (p. 34).

This insistence on confidentiality encouraged the development of what Hollingsworth (1992) terms as a *commitment to the relational process*. Hollingsworth found in her new teacher group that this commitment to the development of trusting relationships "made it possible for teachers to develop their own voices and their own understanding of the issues" (p. 399). In addition to the immense importance of confidentiality, we also found that allowing teachers to determine the content and substance of the group problem-solving discussions was critical in providing support to new teachers.

Agenda set by participants. Most of the teachers claimed that they regularly attended the group meetings because they felt the discussions were pertinent to them both personally and professionally. Since the discussion topics arose from the real-life challenges of the group members, there was a strong consensus that the sessions were "helpful," "interesting," and "relevant" to them. For example, one of the teachers, Rob, a fourth-grade teacher, compared the New Teacher Group meetings with the mentoring group meetings he was required to attend by his school district:

> [The New Teacher Group] was a lot different from the group we had for the mentor stuff. That group was really condescending. Because they were just telling us how to teach, basically, . . . if you were somebody who had just graduated and got a job, it was stuff that you just finished learning in college. It was a big waste of time.

Consistent with our findings from the group interviews, other researchers also discovered that the nature and quality of the teachers' discussions in their groups differed greatly from those conversations that occurred in other circumstances—like student teaching or in-service workshops—where there was an overemphasis on predetermined curricular, academic, and/or administrative concerns (Harris, 1995; Hollingsworth, 1992; Meyer, 1999). We do not claim that everything discussed at each meeting was exactly what each and every teacher needed or felt they needed at that time. It does seem, however, that many of the teachers in the groups believed that the conversations were valuable even when they did not relate exactly to their current problems, issues, or interests. According to a first-grade teacher, Bonnie, what was most helpful about the group was,

> just having somebody to talk to about my problems . . . hearing a variety of solutions. Even when you have to sit and listen to other people's problems, it just brought different things into perspective and [got me] thinking, "Gosh, this could be me!"

Another teacher, Annette, a combination third- and fourth-grade teacher, also felt that the group discussions were pertinent to her even when they did not directly address one of her current needs or interests. She claimed that "All of the topics were really relevant. I never felt there was anything we talked about that . . . I couldn't apply to what I was doing." Finally, Victoria, a fifth-grade teacher, said she valued the group discussions because they also brought out issues she may have to face in the future. Victoria reported that she believed "every discussion was worthwhile even if it was something that had never happened in my room. It at least made me think—if it did happen, how would I handle it?" This is exactly the type of reflection and anticipatory guidance that we hoped to encourage in the New Teacher Groups.

Through focusing the discussions on what Hollingsworth (1992) calls "common practice-based concerns" the teachers were able to talk about problems and issues that emerged from their common experiences as opposed to only those suggested by external theory. Hollingsworth, in her group with new teachers, also focused on issues derived from practice and found that the teachers gained a "greater depth of understanding" and were not "overwhelmed by new information that was irrelevant to their current needs" (p. 399). She emphasizes that theory was not abandoned but instead examples from practice were later abstracted into theoretical frameworks. We also found that because the group discussions were based on the teachers' current experiences and needs, the conversations were especially rich and extremely thoughtful. Often the discussions would progress from a practical concern to a broader abstract or theoretical level, and then return to a practical discussion as the teachers talked about how to address the issue of concern.

The relevancy, frankness, and thoughtful nature of the teachers' problem-solving discussions transformed the biweekly group meetings into a laboratory-like setting where teachers routinely explored and experimented with their ideas about teaching and about themselves as teachers. The quality and depth of the discussions in the New Teacher Groups, as opposed to standard induction activities for beginning teachers, is closely related to the distinction between inquiry-oriented professional development and traditional workshop methods of professional development as discussed by Meyer (1999) and reviewed earlier in this book. Much like the participants in the New Teacher Groups, the teachers in Meyer's group, STEP+, also negotiated the agendas for their meetings, brought problems and issues of their choosing to the group, and jointly decided upon which experiences to discuss, postpone, or forgo. Meyer points out the value of this "generative content" for encouraging conversation and experimentation (p. 231). He suggests that the teachers' conversations were lively, relevant, and challenging because the beginning teacher group he worked with, like our own groups, was "owned and operated" by the teachers (p. 232).

In addition to the value of allowing teachers the opportunity to generate their own content for discussion and experimentation, Hollingsworth (1992) also highlighted the importance of recognizing teachers' experiences in the classroom as valid and important knowledge. By valuing their "experiences and emotions as knowledge," Hollingsworth claimed that she and the teachers in her group were able to "take risks, expose our mistakes, and learn from the emotion and confusion of facing difficult issues" (pp. 399-400). By engaging in this valuing process teachers were encouraged "to raise contextual and theoretical concerns to a level of publicly validated knowledge" (p. 400). As a result, teachers then "see themselves as knowledgeable" and are more likely to develop their own voices as professionals (p. 400). We also saw this process unfold as the teachers helped each other through issues. Valuing teachers' expertise by encouraging them to help their peers seemed to validate their own experiences in the classroom.

In the next section we discuss how, by thoughtfully and sensitively guiding the meetings, the facilitators were able to provide "opportunities to ask questions and reflect upon feedback from broad and welcoming questions." This is another structural feature that Hollingsworth (1992) felt was essential for the support of teachers learning within collaborative conversations (p. 399). The nonevaluative nature of this facilitation encouraged the teachers to talk about their work and themselves as teachers in ways that they could not in other settings or situations.

Nonevaluative facilitators. The groups simply could not have functioned as a safe place where new teachers could talk seriously and honestly about their personal and professional concerns without the presence of facilitators who had no power to evaluate their teaching performance. Without responsive and concerned outsiders facilitating the groups, the discussions would most likely have focused only on technical issues rather than on personal or political concerns. The teachers believed that the meetings would also have turned into "gripe sessions" or "bitch sessions" with little or no focus if there had not been a facilitator to help guide the discussion in a more constructive fashion. According to another group participant, Amanda, who taught second grade, the facilitators were able to "get us back on track to what the problem was and what was happening, rather than letting someone go on and on about how this was a problem and then go off on a million tangents." As with the new teacher groups of Reiman, Bostick, Lassiter, & Cooper (1995), the role of the facilitators in our New Teacher Groups was to listen carefully to the new teachers and then both support and challenge them. In our groups, like in Meyer's (1999) STEP+ beginning teacher group, the "facilitators 'pushed' beyond the 'logistical' to the 'theoretical.' [They] 'listened' responsively and 'summarized'" (p. 232). According to Meyer, the facilitators' role in modeling the behaviors while guiding the discussions helped the new teachers validate their ideas and enhanced their understanding of their practice. The facilitators in our groups also encouraged the presenting teachers to think more deeply about their teaching by posing questions and assisting the teachers in their efforts to reframe their own questions, which helped these teachers further analyze, reconceptualize, and redefine their problems.

Questions were the primary tool used by the facilitators and the teachers to assist the presenting teacher in better understanding their teaching. Rob, a fourth-grade teacher, explained how the facilitators' questions helped encourage thoughtful discussions in the group:

> I think you [facilitators] asked some really good questions. I mean
> it's not like you are just sitting there passing the time away. You

are really seriously thinking about what's going on and you're able to ask really specific questions. . . . All the questions you asked really made me think. And especially when I was listening to other people talking too. Like, wow, that is really a good point. I never even thought about that. I might think about this a little bit. So definitely, it forced me to think more and opened a few doors for me.

Participating in the group's collaborative conversations encouraged the teachers to gain a deeper understanding of their teaching and to realize that it was acceptable for them to have their own ideas about education that differed from standard school beliefs. Hollingsworth (1992) claimed that this process would not have been possible in "an apprentice-type teacher education setting where beginning teachers were viewed as novices by definition" (p. 400). The nonevaluative role of the group facilitators was essential in promoting the teachers' sense of their own voice. Another critical feature of the groups was that they were made up entirely of novices to the profession.

Groups comprised of only beginning teachers. Hollingsworth (1992), Meyer (1999), and Reiman et al. (1995) attest to the value of ensuring that new teachers have the chance to talk to one another on a regular basis in a nonevaluative setting. In our exit interviews, the teachers mentioned again and again the importance of having the groups made up of all beginning teachers. The participating teachers overwhelmingly stated that the single most valuable attribute of the New Teacher Groups was that it offered the opportunity to engage in dialogue with other new teachers. The groups helped to lessen their feelings of isolation as illustrated below by the comments of Darren, a K-5 physical education teacher. Darren claimed that he regularly attended the group "just to talk with someone who was going through what I was going through and hear how they were dealing with it."

It seems that by talking about their problems and listening to peers discuss their concerns, these teachers were better able to put their own situations into perspective. The importance of being in the "same boat" and experiencing similar problems, issues, and dilemmas was a prevalent theme. Sybil, a third grade teacher, expressed this clearly:

I think most helpful was the idea that everybody there had experience [or] was experiencing what I was going through. . . . So I wasn't talking to people about some ethereal problem. They seemed to understand what I was saying and really tried to find a way for me to fix it.

The opportunity to meet with and hear from other first-year colleagues also provided a sense of camaraderie and commitment to other teachers that these beginners could not find anywhere else. Another New Teacher Group member, Lucille, who taught third grade, described the importance of engaging in serious dialogue about teaching with other novice teachers:

> I think the most important part about the group was just the fact that I know people are going through the same things—the camaraderie.... I think that just having a universal sense of new teachers, and new teachers being out there, kind of makes you feel less vulnerable and that helps you.

Indeed, one of the characteristics of effective self-help groups frequently cited in the counseling literature is the notion of universality. Universality, as one of Yalom's (1995) therapeutic factors, is the idea that you are not alone in your problems. This was an important factor in helping the new teachers feel a commitment to the group process.

Meyer (1999) and Hollingsworth (1992) assert the value of peer discussion groups for novices because both claim that the unidirectional nature of mentoring discourages the development of autonomy in new teachers. Novices can only find their voice as teachers through the realization that it is acceptable to have their own ideas about teaching—even if their ideas are different from traditional school beliefs and practices. While useful in some ways, the asymmetrical and unidirectional nature of mentoring threatens the development of "collaborative cultures" and professional conversations between teachers. Groups like the New Teacher Group, on the other hand, encouraged possibilities for developing "collaborative cultures" in schools (Meyer, 1999).

Five Important Group Characteristics
Teachers from different schools. Although the teachers liked talking with others who were in similar situations, they also mentioned the importance of having other new teachers from several different schools in a group. Many of the teachers felt more comfortable talking about the personal, political, and philosophical differences they had with their school administrations, their mentors, or other teachers at their school knowing that they were safe from political or social repercussions. In addition, because the groups members were teachers from various schools in the region,

they broadened each other's understanding of the teaching profession by talking about the similarities and differences between the policies, procedures, and the cultures of the various schools.

By thoughtfully and responsively talking and listening to each other, the teachers in Hollingsworth's (1992) group, much like the teachers in our New Teacher Groups, began "valuing their biographical differences" that enabled them to better "understand, appreciate, and even celebrate both [their] connections and [their] differences" (p. 400). The knowledge and new understanding gained about their colleagues' experiences and practices had important implications both for "the understanding of teachers' work with increasingly diverse populations" and for broadening their conception of teaching as a profession (p. 400).

Having groups composed of teachers from different schools also further ensured that confidentiality was even less likely to be breached. As Janet, a fourth/fifth grade teacher, explained, "It was nice not to be from the same school. You didn't have the sense of cliques that form and your allegiances to certain people. I think confidentiality would have been a much bigger issue." Another factor contributing to forming trusting relationships and providing continuity to the discussions was holding meetings frequently and at regularly scheduled times.

Frequently and consistently held meetings. The fact that the groups met on a regular basis throughout the year was important in terms of the continuity of the discussions and in the formation of trusting relationships. Reiman et al. (1995) also attest to the importance of the "continuity" of regularly held meetings over the course of the school year. The regularity of the meetings provided an opportunity for teachers to really get to know one another, which, in turn, led to the further development of "a commitment to the relational process" (Hollingsworth, 1992, pp. 399-400). Meeting more frequently than every other week would have been particularly difficult for these already overwhelmed new teachers. However, biweekly meetings seemed to encourage the sense of community needed to create a trusting and accepting atmosphere within the groups. As Annette, a combination third- and fourth-grade teacher, explained,

> One thing that I liked is the consistency—every two weeks. Because it is so easy to get busy and to let options not be a priority. It really helped me feel a commitment to the group since it was scheduled so regularly and because it wasn't a month between sessions. I liked the regularity of it.

Although we seldom were able to talk about all that everyone wanted to discuss in our meetings, meeting for an hour and a half or two hours usually provided enough time for two or three in-depth problem-solving discussions. Since we did meet every two weeks, discussions like Janet's, a fifth-grade teacher, would sometimes continue over two or more sessions, which led to more depth and possibilities for even greater understanding. It was obvious then that the frequency and continuity of the meetings encouraged rich discussions. Additionally, for many of the teachers, the predictable format of the groups turned out to be important. It helped them to know what to expect and thus enhanced their focus on the content and their willingness to participate in the discussions.

Predictable format. Clearly what was most valuable to the new teachers was the chance to engage in meaningful dialogue with one another. These discussions were made possible by the way the group meetings were structured. Each teacher was given a short time to share a recent positive and/or negative experience of their choosing. Then two or three teachers volunteered to discuss their specific problems in more detail. The other teachers in the group assisted the presenting teachers in gaining a deeper understanding of their concerns and then provided them with multiple options for addressing the problem. Most of the teachers appreciated the simultaneous structure and informality of the group meetings; they also liked having the opportunity to discuss timely problems as opposed to focusing the discussions on predetermined topics. Craig, a fifth-grade teacher, explained it this way:

> I enjoyed it being informal but I wouldn't have wanted it to be too informal. I was a little hesitant in the beginning thinking that if we got together it was going to be a complaint session. I wouldn't have enjoyed that or gotten much out of that. So it was good to have it structured so . . . people could blow off steam and get support. But it [also] moved into "What are you going to do now?" and to brainstorming. Rather than just coming out with a complaint, people were asking, "What are you going to do about it? What is the solution?" That was good. I think we all needed that.

Another teacher, Maria, a first-grade teacher, described in more detail the importance of the flexibility of the group structure:

> Well, the most helpful thing was the set-up—the way that after we each went around and told something positive, then everybody

kind of focused on those people that had the most pressing problems at the time, rather than saying, "OK, next week is your turn to talk and next week is your turn to talk."

Like Meyer (1999), we found that the structure of the group meetings with its well-known rituals, routines, and roles played an integral part in encouraging thoughtful and relevant discussions. Central to the structure of our meetings was the problem-solving process that encouraged in-depth discussions through the relevance and immediacy of the problems, good questioning by the facilitators and the group members, and a chance to brainstorm possible solutions. It seems that some form of "problem-solving discussion" is important, but, as illustrated by Harris (1995), Hollingsworth (1992), and Meyer (1999), it may take a variety of forms. The main point is that meetings are structured in such a way to encourage the participating teachers to discuss their teaching experiences. Another more practical feature of the New Teacher Group meetings that appeared to encourage attendance was that the teachers were not required to prepare anything ahead of time in order to fully participate in the group discussion.

No outside preparation. Because we knew about the tremendous stress and time constraints associated with the first year of teaching, we made a deliberate decision not to require the teachers to do any outside work to prepare for our New Teacher Group meetings. We felt the teachers could engage in meaningful and productive dialogue without requiring the extra burden of outside preparation. As one of the group participants, Sara, a third grade teacher, suggested, the teachers seemed to appreciate that they didn't "have to bring anything or do anything" to prepare for the meetings. Laura, a new first-grade teacher, also really liked the fact the meetings were "low maintenance" because she didn't have to prepare for them. Paul, a first-grade teacher, claimed that the meetings were useful because "I felt like I was planning or something, yet I didn't have the stress of planning." Annette, a combination third- and fourth-grade teacher, explained why she felt that it was important not to require new teachers to do any preparation for the group meetings. When asked if there was anything that we could do to make the group more helpful Annette responded,

No, I really feel very satisfied with it overall. Yes, there are lots of things you could do, but then it would become much more of a burden to go [to the group meetings]. I mean, yes, it would be nice if I had an article to share with everybody based on what we were talking about—but then that becomes a burden and that is not why I came. The reason I came was because all I had to do was show up. So I think there are lots of things you could do but they would be burdensome and take away the effectiveness.

We are not suggesting that having teachers participate in gathering data about their own teaching or reading research on teaching is not important. The excellent work of Cochran-Smith and Lytle (1993) attests to the power of teachers engaging in intentional, systematic inquiry. Unless, however, teachers are provided with the release time to participate in action research, we believe these activities may be better suited for teachers after their first or second year. Having the meetings in the teachers' classroom also turned out to be symbolic for the respect that was afforded each teacher, thus enhancing his or her sense of professionalism.

Meetings held in participating teachers' classrooms. Mainly for the sake of convenience, we decided to have our meetings in the classrooms of the teachers who participated in the groups. This turned out, however, to be as good a curricular decision as it was a logistic one. The teachers enjoyed seeing the arrangement of their colleagues' classrooms and browsing through their books and teaching materials. Exploring the classrooms was so important to the teachers that we formalized the process as a way to open many of the meetings. The host-teacher appeared to gain as much as the other teachers by leading a guided tour of the room and by explaining her current projects, schedule, and the various books and materials she used in her classroom. One of the second grade teachers, Tracy, claimed that visiting other people's classrooms was valuable because "one of the neatest things to do as a teacher is to go observe other classes." Mark a first-grade teacher, remarked that visiting other teacher's rooms was something that he and other new teachers wanted to do but felt they never had the time or opportunity to do. Mark commented that few first-year teachers are afforded the chance to visit, explore, and ask questions about their colleagues' classrooms, even after the children have gone home, because of time constraints and the ever-present influence of the "culture of teachers" (Britzman, 1986). Finally, many of the new teachers believed that going to the different schools and seeing different classroom settings expanded their understanding of the various ways people approach teaching children and thus helped them develop as teachers.

Summary

By encouraging dialogue and offering a regularly scheduled opportunity to interact with other beginning teachers in a safe and welcoming environment, the New Teacher Groups provided social and emotional support for many first-year teachers. The teachers claimed to have greater knowledge of their teaching and of themselves as teachers by talking and listening to each other, while also broadening their conception of the teaching profession, and forming stronger relationships with their colleagues. They learned how to talk to and work with each other to address problems and issues that may have otherwise never been discussed and dealt with in a thoughtful manner. Hollingsworth's (1992) work also suggests that groups like the New Teacher Group do more than just provide social support, enhance professional growth, personal understanding, and the development of professional identities, as important as these may be. In her longitudinal research project on learning to teach literacy, Hollingsworth found deeper social structures that allowed for what she called "the development of collaborative conversations as epistemic support for beginning teachers as they learn to teach" (p. 399). We believe that the "structural features" described throughout this chapter support the possibilities for thoughtful discussions among teachers that in turn encourage the process of learning to teach. Furthermore, many of these features support the development of habits and attitudes that beginning teachers will carry with them into their schools. Once teachers are afforded the chance to engage in meaningful dialogue with their peers, we feel they will be much more likely to participate in other problem-based discussion groups in the future. They even may serve as agents to disrupt the "culture of teachers" in their schools and school districts (Britzman, 1986). Collaborative conversations focusing on relevant pedagogical issues are more likely than not to arise and take hold in schools where teachers have had the chance to engage in thoughtful discussions about their work.

We will now summarize the main findings from our New Teacher Groups and broaden our scope to discuss how these groups could complement other programs for beginning teachers. We end with a discussion of some conceptual and logistic strategies that would help ease the transition from student to teacher.

Chapter 8

A Comprehensive Support Program
for Beginning Teachers

> **Rob, a fourth-grade teacher:** [One way that the group had an impact on me was that] it made me realize that I can't totally rely on myself. . . . Just because I think I have tried and exhausted every avenue in dealing with a situation does not mean that there aren't other avenues available, so I'm not afraid to turn to somebody; that's for sure.

One of our goals for the New Teacher Groups was to establish a caring professional culture in which teachers felt that they did not have to work through all the problems of the first year alone. Rob's comments suggest that the groups help construct a "culture of collaboration." We believe that teachers will take this collaborative spirit with them and re-create the process throughout their careers. Based on our work of the past several years, we are convinced that problem-based discussion groups like our New Teacher Group not only support teachers during their induction year but also help to determine "what kind of teacher they become" (Feiman-Nemser, 1983, p. 158). This type of learner-centered, collaborative professional development is an essential but typically neglected component for assisting beginning teachers as they navigate the turbulent and often uncharted waters of the first year of teaching.

This final chapter is divided into two parts. In the first part, we highlight three important lessons we learned from the teachers in our

83

groups. We also include a section describing some of the barriers we encountered in implementing our groups. In the second part we focus on other methods for supporting new teachers. We include this because while we believe in the necessity of the New Teacher Groups, we also know that they work best within a supportive school context that complements the kind of collaborative professional development that this book has emphasized.

Three Key Lessons

There are three main lessons that we believe are central to the promotion of more humane, responsive, and proactive forms of professional development for teachers. First, it is clear that teachers need to be active participants in their own professional development. Second, intentional, regularly scheduled peer conversations about teaching practices serve to address many of the social, emotional, and pedagogical needs of beginning teachers. Third, the New Teacher Groups provide a forum that facilitates collaboration with other colleagues in the teaching profession.

Teacher Participation Is Essential to Professional Growth
Facilitated conversation groups that include the teacher as an active, empowered participant are 180 degrees different from the traditional professional development workshop approach. In traditional forms of professional development all participants are treated as passive recipients and assumed to need the same type of support. The unidirectional nature of traditional forms of staff development preclude opportunities for new teachers to gain their voice. In consultee-centered consultation, the emphasis is on helping teachers develop professionally by actively engaging them in the process. Although we found Caplan & Caplan's (1993) model uniquely suited for supporting teachers in this type of professional development, other learner-centered models or frameworks may also work well, as demonstrated by the teacher groups conducted by Meyer (1999), Hollingsworth (1992,) and Harris (1995). Part of what allows the teacher to be a central figure in our approach as well as in these other approaches is the regularly scheduled, facilitated structure of the meetings as discussed in the next section.

The Importance of Talking with Peers
It is not just the opportunity to talk with other teachers that is important

to novices, but rather, it is the chance to engage in regularly scheduled conversations in structured, facilitated meetings with other new teachers. We found that other beginning teachers serve an important role in the professional development of their fellow teachers. Vygotsky's (1978) notion of the Zone of Proximal Development (ZPD) has been promoted since it pairs new teachers with expert teachers. Revisiting Vygotsky, Hertzog (2000) asserts that professional development programs should consider the value of pairing "slightly more expert" teachers (as opposed to "expert" mentor teachers) with the novice. In our experience with the New Teacher Groups, it was clear that the multiple perspectives provided by the group members served as support for learning and professional development. Although all the members of the group were beginning teachers, they were not all at the same level of competence and understanding in all the domains of teaching practice at any one time. For example, in one of our groups, one teacher felt particularly competent in the area of classroom management, while another was especially proud of her reading program, while another had experience with special needs children. What is salient here is that the new teachers were able to serve as "experts" for each other in different areas of practice. This served two purposes. First, the potential for teachers to socially construct (or coconstruct) meaning was present in the group problem-solving discussions as the new teachers shared their knowledge and their expertise with their colleagues, that is conversing with colleagues who had a deeper understanding of the issues discussed enhanced the teachers' learning. Second, the opportunity to share their knowledge with others had a positive impact on the new teachers' sense of professionalism and competence.

What happened, then, in our New Teacher Groups, in terms of Vygotsky's (1978) notion of the Zone of Proximal Development, was that the role of the more-experienced other rotated among the members of the group. The multiple perspectives offered by the group members afforded the presenting teacher the chance to see her problem in a new light. This process is thus consistent with Vygotsky's concept of socially constructed meaning, yet departs from the usual application of Vygotsky where there is one expert, or a static hierarchy of expert/novice. In our groups, because the role of expert was evolving and shared, these new teachers were, in effect, mentoring each other.

The Value of Learning to Collaborate
Adding to the difficulties faced by beginning teachers in our present-day

schools are the complications and consequences of living in postmodern times. According to Hargreaves (1994), the fast pace and complexity of the postmodern world "is presenting immense problems and challenges" for schools and teachers alike. He believes that critical to addressing these problems is the need to create new "collaborative modes of decision making" to break the "norms of teacher isolation in which teachers' work has been based" (pp. 9-10).

Hargreaves (1994) insists that the need to learn how to collaborate is crucial so that the new social structure of teaching progresses from that of "individualism" to a "professional community" (p. 20). As more schools move toward school-based governance it is necessary for teachers to have the ability and motivation to participate in collaborative team efforts toward school reform. Our findings suggest that the New Teacher Group meetings provide a vehicle for beginning teachers to learn how to collaborate with their fellow teachers. Thus the groups give them the opportunity to "practice" collaboration skills that they can take to their schools and use when working with their colleagues.

Lieberman and Miller (1999) also claim that schools must adapt to meet the challenges they term the *new social realities of teaching* that include

- dealing with conflict

- thinking systemically

- including everyone

- using and sharing ideas

- working bottom-up and top-down

- keeping perspectives amid the confusion.

As important as it is for teachers to learn to work together, we must not, however, lose sight of the fact that the primary goal in supporting teacher's development in collaborative consultation groups is to improve their teaching. As Shulman (1999) states,

> Teacher collegiality and collaboration are not important merely for the improvement of morale and teacher satisfaction (which always sound like a lame argument in favor of satisfied teachers,

regardless of whether they succeed in teaching kids); they are absolutely necessary if teaching is to be of the highest order and thus compatible with the standards of excellence demanded by the recent reforms. (p. 167)

Keeping in mind the important lessons we learned from our work with the New Teacher Groups, we move to the next section where we discuss some of the difficulties we encountered in providing this opportunity to beginning teachers. In the final section, we broaden our scope of recommendations for assisting these teachers.

Barriers to Providing Support for New Teachers

In this section, we discuss some of the challenges that we encountered in conducting our New Teacher Groups over the past several years. While some of these barriers may be specific to our setting and circumstances, others are common concerns that educators might encounter in providing this type of professional development for beginning teachers.

Time and logistics. Time is probably one of beginning teachers' most precious commodities, as teaching for the first time takes a tremendous amount of planning and preparation. In addition, many of these teachers are already overcommitted with extracurricular activities, faculty meetings, and meetings with parents. For the small number of teachers who dropped out of the New Teacher Groups, time was often cited as the main reason why they could not continue to participate.

The location of the meeting can be another logistic challenge. We held our group meetings in a different teacher's classroom each week; this provided an opportunity for everyone to see how others organized their classrooms. While most new teachers appreciated seeing a range of classrooms, meeting in a different location each time can be somewhat confusing. We provided maps to each of the school sites and sometimes made reminder phone calls about the location of the meeting. For some of the groups, starting the meeting on time was also a continuing struggle because of the teachers' other after school commitments or the distance they needed to travel to get to the meetings. Once New Teacher Groups become an institutionalized part of the school culture, however, issues of time and logistics may become less of a barrier. Along these lines, the need for administrative support is discussed in the next section.

Administrative support. It may be difficult for some administrators to appreciate the value of extended periods of self-reflection and group discussion among beginning teachers. This approach is very different than "professional-development-as-usual" and it may be necessary to educate principals, superintendents, and school boards about the value of this type of support. One way to establish groups as a legitimate and meaningful professional development activity is to include it as part of the orientation program for beginning teachers. Administrators could further legitimize participation in such groups by offering teachers continuing education credit (which is often required to renew their teaching licenses).

Another area in which administrators can be helpful is by providing funding to pay the group facilitators. In our case, our research was funded by a private foundation so that the facilitators were paid from a source outside the school. However, in order to maintain the groups over a long period of time it would be essential to have some school funding. Finding appropriate group facilitators can also be a challenge, as discussed in the next section.

Recruiting, training, and supervising group facilitators. In addition to finding money to support the New Teacher Groups, it may be difficult to find individuals who are willing and able to serve as group facilitators. As stated earlier, the facilitators need to be knowledgeable about education and about the process of consultation, in addition to having excellent interpersonal skills. Furthermore, the facilitators should have no evaluative power over the new teachers. While many principals would likely be effective group leaders, because of their position of authority they would not a good choice for a New Teacher Group facilitators. We started out training graduate students to serve as group facilitators for our project but also expanded to include former group members as co-leaders as well as some experienced teachers. Other school personnel who might be well suited to conduct the groups would be the school counselor, the school psychologist, or perhaps a supervisor of curriculum and instruction.

Regardless of the background of the facilitators, it is important to provide training in the group consultation process to these facilitators before they begin their own group. As stated earlier, one of the biggest challenges for facilitators is to resist the pressure to provide quick solutions and to solve the teachers' problems. Training in consultation skills provides the facilitators with a framework to follow in the problem-solving process.

As the facilitators deal with the dynamics of the group, supervision and/or consultative support is essential. We have found that the facilitators benefit from the opportunity to talk with each other about challenging situations that arise in the groups. Some of these challenges will be discussed in the next section.

Issues of race, culture, and gender. Differences in culture, race, religion, ethnicity, language, and gender are important issues in schools as well as in society at large. This is an issue that merits book-length discussion but is also very dependent on the context of each situation. For example, in one of our groups racial conflicts in the teacher's classroom and among the participants of the group became a concern. Gender issues both within the group and in the workplace are potentially volatile issues that need to be handled with skill and sensitivity. Young female teachers may feel that they have difficulty establishing themselves as authority figures with some of the children's parents. One of the male teachers in our groups talked about how the physical contact with students that the female teachers take for granted, such as touching a child's shoulder, or hugging a child, can be misinterpreted if done by a man. Gay and lesbian teachers and/or parents may be another issue that teachers would discuss. Working with students and adults from other cultures, who speak languages other than English is often a concern for new teachers. Teachers may have strong feelings about these issues that may be in conflict with their institution's values. The New Teacher Groups could be an effective forum for the discussion of these sensitive issues. Group facilitators should be alerted to these possible areas of concern although ongoing consultative support is probably most effective as they address these issues in their groups.

While the New Teacher Groups are an important form of inquiry-oriented professional development, they should be considered as one element in a more comprehensive induction year program. In the next section, we offer suggestions for other approaches that complement problem-based discussion groups and may serve to ease the transition from student to teacher.

Supporting the Development of Beginning Teachers with a Comprehensive Induction Program

The New Teacher Groups are just one in an array of things we need to do to assist teachers in their first year. There are few, if any, other professions that treat their novices as callously as we do our first-year teachers. Although educators have been aware of the difficulties faced by new teachers for many years, we continue to set the teachers up for failure by not providing them with ample support. These teachers are expected to do the same work as their seasoned colleagues often in more difficult circumstances with less equipment, fewer supplies, and no job experience. What makes this even worse, is that new teachers are typically expected to do this by themselves in a classroom often far away from a mentor and with children that other teachers did not want in their classes. To illustrate what we mean here, it might be instructive to envision a parallel situation in another profession. The medical profession would never allow an analogous situation to occur with a doctor just out of medical school. Imagine a new MD entering a hospital on the first day of her residency in surgery. She reports to the chief administrator at the hospital who immediately says,

> I'm so glad you are here because we have a patient who has been waiting a long time for open-heart surgery. None of the other doctors want to perform it because he is such a high-insurance risk. So I'd like you to perform this operation yourself. I realize you are just out of medical school and you don't have any surgical tools or equipment, but I purchased this brand-new Boy Scout knife for you. You see, all of the scalpels are being use by the more experienced surgeons who, by the way, also have reserved all of the operating theaters and all of the available anesthesiologists. But don't worry; we have a nice clean table in the waiting room where you can perform your operation. And we have lots and lots of aspirin to give to your patient after surgery to help relieve his pain.

Although this example may seem extreme, we do not think it is very different from what we do to many of our first-year teachers in schools. As mentioned earlier, all too often these teachers are assigned the most difficult teaching situations with little or no support. In order to truly assist teachers in the early years in the profession we need to provide a variety of human and logistic support strategies.

As Rebecca, a third-grade teacher, states, the first year of teaching "[was] very difficult and I think a lot of it didn't have to happen." She and many of the other teachers believed that much of the grief and stress they suffered would not have been so great if they had been better supported by their school administration and by their more experienced colleagues. We offer some suggestions that we believe may be beneficial to the development and support of first-year teachers. Again, these suggestions represent an array of possible strategies for assisting new teachers—one of which, of course, is providing them with opportunities to engage in frequent practice-based discussions with each other.

Human and Logistic Support from School Administrators

In order for new teachers to have the social and emotional support necessary to do their job well while simultaneously developing as professionals, they need both human and logistic support from their school and district administrators. This starts with an attentive and caring principal, a principal who is available and willing to listen and to engage in frequent problem-solving conversations with his or her new teachers. The principal can also assist beginning teachers by providing logistic support and by working to create a school culture where helping these teachers is the norm.

A good example of how administrative leadership can create a supportive climate designed to help beginning teachers can be found in a high school in North Carolina. Each summer the staff at the school invites their first-year teachers to an orientation that takes place before the required teacher workdays. The new teachers' mentors are present along with the school administrators. These teachers are given a tour of the school, the school board offices, and the town in an attempt not only to orient them geographically but to help them more easily locate human and material resources they may need as teachers. The mentors and administrators help the new teachers design their rooms, locate and order educational materials, and answer their questions about the school's policies and procedures. Mentors then work with these teachers to help them set up their classrooms and develop thoughtful approaches to classroom management and discipline. Finally, these mentors work together with the beginning teachers to write detailed lesson plans for their first day of school and then help them outline their plans for the rest of the first week. This kind of assistance and support is invaluable for beginning teachers; the first year would be much less traumatic if other schools would initiate their novices in this manner.

Importance of a Good Mentor

In addition to helping new teachers before school starts, the principal can also be instrumental in providing support for these teachers throughout their first year by assigning them a carefully chosen mentor. At least half of the new teachers in our groups claimed that their mentors were of no help at all. Many of the novice teachers never even talked to their mentors after their initial meetings with them. A good mentor needs to be available to answer questions and help with all kinds of problems—from logistic problems such as how to order supplies and how to fill out a field-trip request form to more political and pedagogical problems such as how to conduct a conference with an overly demanding parent and how to differentiate instruction to ensure that all the children are interested and learning.

Done well, mentoring is a sophisticated and complex form of teaching requiring strong collaboration, critical reflection, and excellent interpersonal skills. Thus, we believe that mentors, like new teachers, could also profit from their own problem-based discussion group focusing on issues they encountered while working with their assigned novice teachers. Furthermore, it should be recognized that mentoring is a time-consuming responsibility. For instance, in some districts in Oregon, mentor teachers are released from their classroom duties to work exclusively with a small group of new teachers for the entire school year. This kind of administrative and institutional support is a basic but often overlooked ingredient in mentoring programs.

Support for Working with Adults
As noted earlier, one of the greatest concerns of the new teachers was the difficulty that often occurs in interactions with other adults, particularly teaching assistants and parents. In North Carolina, kindergarten through third-grade teachers have an assistant in their classroom at least part of the day. These assistants were often twenty to twenty-five years older than the beginning teachers and had ten or more years of experience in the classroom. Although there are many excellent teaching assistants, there are also those who have developed rigid routines and negative ways of interacting with children. It is extremely difficult for a young, new teacher to work collaboratively with an older, more experienced co-teacher because the power relationship may be weighted in favor of the older, more experienced assistant teacher. Most new teachers have had little, if any experience in a role where they had to act more like the boss than the employee.

This lack of experience and the power differential also comes into play when the new teacher is thrust into the role of expert and is forced to deal with parents who are often older, may have more "real world" experience, and may have a cultural perspective different from the new teacher. Principals need to choose mentors, teaching assistants, or co-teachers who are flexible, communicative, and can collaborate well with those new to the teaching profession. It is also important for principals to provide opportunities for new teachers to learn how to communicate with parents and how to conduct an effective parent-teacher conference by providing them with formal or informal forums that facilitate their learning how to do so.

Novices as Co-teachers

Districts who are willing to experiment may want to try assigning two first-year teachers to the same classroom. As noted earlier, Vygotskian theory (1978) and lessons we learned through working with the teachers in our groups suggest that pairing two beginning teachers together has the potential for each to teach at a higher level than she or he could if teaching alone. It seems evident that two beginning teachers are much more likely to reach more children than one new teacher could, but we also think that two novices may be more effective instructors than the combination of one new teacher and certain teaching assistants. These new co-teachers could create twice as many instructional materials; co-plan lessons and activities; work more often with individuals and small groups of children; and have someone to talk to, and reflect on, their experiences with children at the end of each school day. We contend that these paired new teachers would feel less isolated and experience a greater sense of support as a result of their opportunity to talk with each other and collaborate daily on meaningful and timely work. Furthermore, our sense is that two carefully selected new teachers would not suffer the same stress as other new teachers working alone, and thus would be more likely to continue in the profession after their initial year. Although the economics of this plan may seem a little suspect on the surface, if in school districts that already have teaching assistants another initially certified teacher was hired instead, it would not cost the district much more in terms of salaries. Additionally, because of the strong possibility that a paired new teacher would be more likely to stay in the profession, it would cost the district less in terms of recruitment and staff development expenditures in the future. The long-term benefits to the children and to the new teachers themselves seem to far outweigh the initial financial differences.

Logistic Strategies for Supporting New Teachers

Some logistic initiatives that district and school administrators could implement to help beginning teachers better cope with the rigors of the first year include:

- assigning lighter teaching loads—smaller classes

- requiring minimal committee work or extracurricular activities

- letting first-year teachers teach in the same grade level and/or the same subject area as they did in their student-teaching practicum

- providing beginning teachers with ample materials and educational supplies

- giving first-year teachers their own classroom (not just assigning them to a temporary space or providing them with a cart so they can move their materials from room to room)

- not assigning the majority of the "most difficult" students to the new teachers

- assigning minimal paperwork and providing assistance for the paper work that is assigned.

The first year of teaching would be much more rewarding and productive for many beginning teachers if these suggestions were implemented by school and district administrators. We believe that if we are to ensure the professional development and support of new teachers it is essential to provide them with an array of support strategies like those just outlined along with some form of inquiry-oriented approach to professional development. We, like Lieberman and Miller (1999), feel that it is critical to offer new teachers professional development opportunities where "prescription and compliance are replaced by a challenging involvement in problem posing, sharing and solving, discussions that concern actions and consequences, and a culture that encourages continuous inquiry" (p. 17). If we are to genuinely encourage new teachers' professional development, we must provide them with venues in which they can begin to make sense of the complicated nature of their work as teachers. Finally, we believe that this can be best facilitated by offering beginning teachers structured, regularly scheduled opportunities to discuss their practice through problem-posing and problem-solving conversations with their peers.

References

Agar, M. H. (1980). *The professional stranger: An informal introduction to ethnography.* New York: Academic.

Anderson, R., Cissna, K. N., & Arnett, R. C. (1994). *The reach of dialogue: Confirmation, voice, and community.* Cresshill, NJ: Hampton Press.

Ashton, P. (1984). Teacher efficacy: A motivational paradigm for effective teacher education. *Journal of Teacher Education, 35*(5), 28–32.

Babinski, L. M., & Rogers, D. L. (1998). Supporting new teachers through consultee-centered group consultation. *Journal of Educational and Psychological Consultation, 9*(4), 285–308.

Bakhtin, M. M. (1981). *The dialogic imagination.* Austin: University of Texas Press.

Banner, J. M., & Cannon H. C. (1997). The "who" of teaching. *Education Week, 56,* 42.

Bell, B., & Gilbert, J. (1994). Teacher development as professional, personal, and social development. *Teaching and Teacher Education, 10,* 483–497.

Bergan, J. R., & Kratochwill, T. R. (1990). *Behavioral consultation and therapy.* New York: Plenum.

Britzman, D. P. (1986). Cultural myths in the making of a teacher: Biography and social structure in teacher education. *Harvard Educational Review, 56*(4), 442–456.

95

Brown, D., Pryzwansky, W., & Schulte, A. (1998). *Psychological consultation: An introduction to theory and practice.* 4th ed. Boston: Allyn.

Brownell, J. (1993). Listening environment: A perspective. In A. D. Wolvin & C. W. Coakley (Eds.), *Perspectives on listening* (pp. 241–260). Norwood, NJ: Ablex.

Brufee, K. (1993). *Collaborative learning: Higher education, interdependence, and the authority of knowledge.* Baltimore, MD: Johns Hopkins University Press.

Bruneau, T. (1993). Empathy and listening. In A. D. Wolvin & C. W. Coakley (Eds.), *Perspectives on listening* (pp. 185–200). Norwood, NJ: Ablex.

Bruner, J. (1986). *Actual minds, possible worlds.* Cambridge: Harvard University Press.

Bullough, R. V. (1987). First year teaching: A case study. *Teachers College Record, 89*(2), 39–46.

Bullough, R. V. (1991). Exploring personal teaching metaphors in preservice teacher education. *Journal of Teacher Education,* 42(1), 43–51.

Bush, R. N. (1965). The formative years. *The real world of the beginning teacher.* Washington, DC: National Commission on Teacher Education and Professional Standards, National Education Association.

Caplan, G. (1974). Support Systems. In G. Caplan (Ed.), *Support systems and community mental health* (pp. 1–40). New York: Basic.

Caplan, G., & Caplan, R. B. (1993). *Mental health consultation and collaboration.* San Francisco: Jossey-Bass.

Caplan, G., Caplan, R. B., & Erchul, W. P. (1995). A contemporary view of mental health consultation: Comments on "Types of mental health consultation" by Gerald Caplan (1963). *Journal of Educational and Psychological Consultation,* 6(1), 23–30.

Cissna, K. N., & Anderson, R. (1994). In Anderson, R., Cissna, K. N., & Arnett, R. C. (Eds.), *The reach of dialogue: Confirmation, voice, and community* (pp. 9–30). Cresshill, NJ: Hampton Press.

Cochran-Smith, M., & Lytle, S. (1993). *Inside/outside: Teacher research and knowledge.* New York: Teachers College Press.

Coles, R. (1989). *The call of stories: Teaching and the moral imagination.* Boston: Houghton.

Collins, P. (1991). *Black feminist thought.* New York: Routledge and Kegan Paul.

Cooper, K. C. (2000, January 13). 'Best and Brightest' leave teaching early, Study says. *Washington Post*, p. A02.

Corcoran, E. (1981). Transition shock: The beginning teacher's paradox. *Journal of Teacher Education*, 36(6), 49–53.

Corcoran, T. (1995). *Transforming professional development for teachers: A guide for state policymakers.* A report prepared for the National Governors' Association. Washington, DC: Center for Policy Research.

Corey, M. S., & Corey, G. (1997). *Groups: Process and practice.* 5th ed. Boston: Brooks/Cole.

Dewey, J. (1933). *How we think: A restatement of the relation of reflective thinking to the educative process.* Chicago: Henry Regnery.

Duckworth, E. (1994). What teachers know: The best knowledge base. *Harvard Educational Review*, 54(1), 15–19.

Featherstone, D., Munby, H., & Russell, T. (Eds.). (1997). *Finding a voice while learning to teach.* London: Fulmer.

Feiman-Nemser, S. (1983). Learning to teach. In L. S. Shulman & G. Skyes (Eds.), *Handbook of teaching and policy* (pp. 150–170). New York: Longman.

Fessler, R., & Christensen, J. C. (1992). *The teacher career cycle: Understanding and guiding the professional development of teachers.* Boston: Allyn.

Friedman, M. (1994). The partnership of existence. In R. Anderson, K. N. Cissna, & R. C. Arnett (Eds.), *The reach of dialogue: Confirmation, voice, and community* (pp. 79–88). Cresshill, NJ: Hampton Press.

Friedman, P. G. (1993). Listening for narrative. In A. D. Wolvin & C. W. Coakley (Eds.), *Perspectives on listening* (pp. 201–216). Norwood, NJ: Ablex.

Fuller, F. F. (1969). Concerns of teachers: A developmental conceptualization. *American Educational Research Journal*, 6(2), 207–226.

Gilroy, P. (1989). Professional knowledge and the beginning teacher. In W. Carr (Ed.), *Quality in teaching: Arguments for reflective practice* (pp. 101–113). London: Falmer Press.

Glassberg, S. (1979). A developmental model for the beginning teacher. In K. Howey & R. Bents (Eds.), *Towards meeting the needs of the beginning teacher* (pp. 111–138). Minneapolis: Midwest Teacher Corps Network and University of Minnesota/St. Paul Schools Teacher Corps Project.

Gomez, M., & Tabachnick, B. R. (1992). Telling teacher stories. *Teaching Education*, 4(2), 129–138.

Goodlad, J. I. (1984). *A place called school*. New York: McGraw-Hill.

Gordon, S. P. (1991). *How to teach beginning teachers to succeed*. Alexandria, VA: Clearinghouse.

Gottlieb, B. J. (1988). Marshalling social support: The state of the art in research and practice. In B. J. Gottlieb (Ed.) *Marshalling social support* (pp. 11–51). Newbury Park, CA: Sage.

Grant, C. A., & Zeichner, K. M. (1981). Inservice support for first-year teachers: The state of the scene. *Journal of Research and Development in Education*, 14(2), 99–111.

Gregorc, A.F., & Ward, H. B. (1977). Implications for teaching and learning: A new definition for individual. *NASSP Bulletin*, 61(406), 20–26.

Hargreaves, A. (1994). *Changing teachers, changing lives: Teachers' work and culture in the postmodern age*. New York: Teachers College Press.

Harris, D. L. (1995). *Composing a life as a teacher: The role of conversation and community in teachers' formation of their identities as professionals*. Unpublished doctoral dissertation, Michigan State University. UMI Dissertation Abstracts, UMI Number 9605874.

Hawk, P. P. (1984). *Reflections and thoughts of first year teachers: Making a difference*. Greenville, NC: East Carolina University.

Hertzog, H. S. (2000, April). *When, how and who do I ask for help? Novices' perceptions of learning and assistance.* Paper presented at the meeting of the American Educational Research Association, New Orleans.

Hollingsworth, S. (1989). Prior beliefs and cognitive change in learning to teach. *American Educational Research Journal,* 26(1), 160–189.

Hollingsworth, S. (1992). Learning to teach through collaborative conversation: A feminist approach. *American Educational Research Journal,* 29(2), 373–404.

Hopkins, P. A. (1996). *The effect of induction interventions on the desire of beginning teachers to remain in teaching.* Unpublished doctoral dissertation, North Carolina State University at Raleigh. UMI Dissertation Abstracts, UMI Number 9708326.

Huling-Austin, L. (1989). A synthesis of research on teacher induction programs and practices. In J. Reinhartz (Ed.), *Teacher Induction* (13–33). Washington, DC: National Education Association.

Huling-Austin, L. (1990). What can and cannot reasonably be expected from teacher induction programs. *Journal of Teacher Education,* 37(1), 2–5.

Huling-Austin, L. (1992). Research on learning to teach: Implications for teacher induction and mentoring programs. *Journal of Teacher Education,* 43(3), 173–180.

Huling-Austin, L., Odell, S., Ishler, P., Kay, R., & Edelfelt, R. (1989). *Assisting the beginning teacher.* Reston, VA: Association of Teacher Educators.

Johnson, L. J., & Pugach, M. C. (1996). Role of collaborative dialogue in teachers' conceptions of appropriate practice for students at risk. *Journal of Educational and Psychological Consultation,* 7(1), 9–24.

Kagan, D. M. (1992). Professional growth among preservice and beginning teachers. *Review of Educational Research,* 62(2), 129–169.

Kestner, J. L. (1994). New teacher induction: Findings of the research and implications for minority groups. *Journal of Teacher Education,* 45(1), 39–45.

Levin, B., & Ammon, P. (1992). The development of beginning teachers' pedagogical thinking: A longitudinal analysis of four case studies. *Teacher Education Quarterly,* Fall, 19–37.

Lieberman, A., & Miller, L. (1984). *Teachers: Their world and their work.* Alexandria, VA: Association for Supervision and Curriculum Development.

Lieberman, A., & Miller, L. (1999). *Teachers: Transforming their world and their work.* Alexandria, VA: Association for Supervision and Curriculum Development.

Lightfoot, S. L. (1983). The lives of teachers. In S. L. Shulman & G. Skyes (Eds.), *Handbook of teaching and policy* (pp. 241–260). New York: Longman.

Lortie, D. C. (1975). *Schoolteacher: A sociological study.* Chicago: University of Chicago Press.

MacIntyre, A. (1981). *After virtue.* Notre Dame, IN: Notre Dame University Press.

Matson, F. W., & Montagu, A. (1967). *The human dialogue: Perspectives on communication.* New York: Free Press.

Merseth, K. K. (1990). *Beginning teachers and computer networks: A new form of induction support* (Report No. 90–9). East Lansing, MI: National Center for Research on Teacher Education. (ERIC Document Reproduction Service No. ED 324 309).

Meyer, T. (1999). *Conversational learning: The role of talk in a novice teacher learning community.* Unpublished doctoral dissertation: Stanford University. Accession No: AAG9943700.

Meyers, J. (1995). A consultation model for school psychological services: Twenty years later. *Journal of Educational and Psychological Consultation*, 6(1), 73–81.

Miles, M. B., & Huberman, A. M. (1994). *Qualitative data analysis.* 2nd ed. Thousand Oaks, CA: Sage.

Munby, H., & Russell, T. (1994). The authority of experience in learning to teach: Messages from a physics methods course. *Journal of Teacher Education*, 45(2), 86–95.

Noddings, N. (1992). *The challenge to care in schools.* New York: Teachers College Press.

Noddings, N., & Witherell, C. (1991). Epilogue: Themes remembered and foreseen. In C. Witherell and N. Noddings (Eds.), *Stories lives tell: Narrative and dialogue in education* (pp. 279–280). New York: Teachers College Press.

Odell, S. J. (1989). Characteristics of beginning teachers in an induction context. In J. Reinhartz (Ed.), *Teacher induction* (pp. 42–51). Washington, DC: National Education Association.

Pierce, K. M., & Gilles, C. J. (1993). *Cycles of meaning: Exploring the potential of talk in learning communities*. Portsmouth, NH: Heinemann.

Powell, J. (1969). *Why am I afraid to tell you who I am?* Niles, IL: Argus.

Purdy, M. (1997). What is listening? In M. Purdy & D. Borisoff (Eds.), *Listening in everyday life: A personal and professional approach* (pp. 1–20). Lanham, MD: University Press of America.

Reiman, A. J., Bostick, D., Lassiter, J., & Cooper, J. (1995). Counselor- and teacher-led support groups for beginning teachers: A cognitive-developmental perspective. *Elementary School Guidance and Counseling*, 30(2), 105–117.

Richert, A. (1992). Voice and power. In L. Valli (Ed.), *Reflective teacher education: Cases and critiques* (pp. 187–197). Albany: State University of New York Press.

Ryan, K. (1970). *Don't smile until Christmas: Accounts of the first year of teaching*. Chicago: University of Chicago Press.

Ryan, K. (1980). *Biting the apple: Accounts of first year teachers*. New York: Longman.

Ryan, K. (1986). *The induction of new teachers*. Phi Delta Kappa Fastback No. 237. Bloomington, IN: Phi Delta Kappa Educational Foundation.

Schatzman, L., & Strauss, A. (1973). *Field research: Strategies for a natural sociology*. Englewood Cliffs, NJ: Prentice Hall.

Schlechty, P.C. (1984, November). *Restructuring the teaching occupation: A proposal*. Paper presented for the American Educational Research Association Project, Research Contributions for Educational Improvement.

Schön, D. A. (1987). *Educating the reflective practitioner*. San Francisco: Jossey-Bass.

Schwab, J. J. (1976). Education and the state: Learning community. *The great ideas today*. Chicago: Encyclopedia Britannica.

Sergiovanni, T. J. (1994). *Building community in schools*. San Francisco: Jossey-Bass.

Shulman, L. S. (1988). Teaching alone, learning together: Needed agendas for the new reforms. In T. J. Sergiovanni and J. H. Moore (Eds.), *Schooling for tomorrow: Directing reforms to issues that count*. Boston: Allyn.

Shulman, L. S. (1999). Taking learning seriously. *Change: The Magazine of Higher Learning*, July/August, 11–17.

Sprinthall, N.A. & Theis-Sprinthall, L. (1983). The teacher as an adult learner: A cognitive development view. In G. Griffin (Ed.) *Staff development: Eighty-second yearbook of the National Society for the Study of Education* (pp. 13–35). Chicago: University of Chicago Press.

Tellez, K. (1992). Mentors by choice, not design: Help-seeking by beginning teachers. *Journal of Teacher Education*, 43(3), 214–221.

Thies-Sprinthall, L. (1986). A collaborative approach for mentor training: A working model. *Journal of Teacher Education*, 37(6), 13–20.

Veenman, S. (1984). Perceived problems of beginning teachers. *Review of Educational Research*, 54(2), 143–178.

Vygotsky, L. S. (1978). *Mind and society: The development of higher psychological processes*. Cambridge: Harvard University Press.

Wardhaugh, R. (1985). *How conversation works*. New York: B. Blackwell.

Wise, A. E., Darling-Hammond, L., & Berry, B. (1987). *Effective teacher selection: From recruitment to retention*. Santa Monica: Rand (No. R–3462–NIE/CSTP).

Yalom, I. D. (1995). *The theory and practice of group psychotherapy*. New York: Basic.

Zins, J. E. (1993). Enhancing consultee problem-solving skills in consultation interactions. *Journal of Counseling and Development*, 72, 185–190.

Zins, J. E., Maher, C. A., Murphy, J. J., & Weiss, B. P. (1988). The peer support group: A means to facilitate professional development. *School Psychology Review*, 17, 138–146.

Zumwalt, K. K. (1982). Research on teaching: Policy implications for teacher education. In A. Lieberman & M. W. McLaughlin (Eds.), *Policymaking in education, 81ˢᵗ yearbook* (pp. 215–248). Chicago: National Society for the Study of Education.

Notes

[1]An earlier version of this problem-solving example appeared in Babinski, L. M., & Rogers, D. L. (1998). Supporting new teachers through consultee-centered group consultation. *Journal of Educational and Psychological Consultation*, 9(4), 285–308.

Appendix A

New Elementary Teacher Group

Why have a new teacher group?

The first year of teaching is an extremely challenging time for most people. One way to help you through this time is to meet regularly with other beginning teachers to talk about your joys and frustrations. For the last three years we conducted new teacher groups that met every other week for a couple of hours. The teachers found talking to each other about their school experiences very valuable. They were able to help each other solve classroom management problems, share teaching ideas, and discuss how to best work with parents and administrators.

What have teachers said about the group?

- "Sometimes just realizing that you're not alone is all you need."

- "Meeting other teachers was neat, but what was also interesting was getting to really listen to colleagues . . . I feel very professional as I leave the meetings full of ideas and thoughts about my career."

- "I was really nice to bounce ideas, frustrations, and questions off of people in the same situation."

- "This group helped answer practical questions about parent relations, referrals, and so forth. The diversity of teaching styles and experiences [within the group] enabled us to come up with an abundance of ideas for solving classroom problems. Most of all it helped me realize that I was not alone."

What will the group be like?

We will be setting up a group of new teachers to meet regularly during this school year beginning in September. The agenda will be decided by the group based on their interests and needs. We'd like to meet every other week for about two hours after school for a total of seven meetings in the fall. Volunteers who wish to participate in this group should be willing to make this time commitment. Each group will be limited to seven beginning elementary teachers from different schools and school districts.

What's in it for the facilitators?

We are interested in helping new teachers and in studying issues that are important to them. We want to learn more about how we can help teachers, and how they can help each other, during their first year of teaching. In order for us to do this, we'll be studying this New Teacher Group. If you decide to join the group, you will become part of our study.

How do I sign up?

Please sign the list today if you're interested in participating. If you have additional questions, please contact Dwight L. Rogers, Ph.D. or Leslie M. Babinski, Ph.D., School of Education, University of North Carolina (UNC) at Chapel Hill.

Appendix B

New Teacher Groups
Field Notes

Facilitator's Name:_____ Date:_____

Time: Begin:_____End:_____   Location:_____

Teachers present:

Sharing time. List what issues were shared with the group.

Problem-solving discussions. Please include the following information: (1) the name of the presenting teacher; (2) a description of the issue; (3) how the teacher framed the problem; (4) how the teachers responded; (5) amount of time spent on the discussion, and (6) any result of the discussion, i.e., teacher's plan of action. Complete one summary sheet for each issue:

Level of participation of each member:

Overall impressions of the meeting (atmosphere, morale, and group cohesiveness)

Issues to be discussed at the next meeting—follow-up:

Please identify topics or issues that should be studied in more detail:

Issue Summary Sheet

Issue 1:_____

Teacher's name:

Amount of time spent on the issue:

Description of the issue:

How the issue was framed (i.e., teacher's problem, child's problem, or school problem):

Description of how the group members responded:

Result of the discussion (i.e. plan of action):

Issue Summary Sheet

Issue 2: _____

Teacher's name:

Amount of time spent on the issue:

Description of the issue:

How the issue was framed (i.e., teacher's problem, child's problem, or school problem):

Description of how the group members responded:

Result of the discussion (i.e. plan of action):

Issue Summary Sheet

Issue 3: _____

Teacher's name:

Amount of time spent on the issue:

Description of the issue:

How the issue was framed (i.e., teacher's problem, child's problem, or school problem):

Description of how the group members responded:

Result of the discussion (i.e. plan of action):

Appendix C
Consent Form for Teacher Support Group

Dear Teacher,

The support group will provide a forum for new elementary schoolteachers to discuss issues and problems that they encounter during their first or second year of teaching. In addition, the facilitators of the group, Dwight L. Rogers and Leslie M. Babinski, will be using information from this group to examine issues important to new teachers and to the process of group support.

Your participation in this project is voluntary and includes biweekly two-hour group meetings with six to eight other teachers from September through June for a total of approximately sixteen sessions. We will audio tape the meetings and we will also be taking notes to document the types of issues that are discussed. We will ask you to provide both verbal and written feedback evaluating the group as a means of support for new teachers. In addition, you will be asked to complete a questionnaire about the group environment in September and June. When we transcribe the tapes, you will be identified only by a code name and the tapes will be kept in a locked file drawer until they are destroyed in two years when the project is completed. Furthermore, when we write about and report on the results of this group, we will not reveal your names, the names of your schools, or any of the names of the students that you mention in the group. In other words, the information collected during the group sessions will remain confidential.

The information you provide may be helpful in determining ways to provide support for new teachers in the future. You may also benefit personally from the group through your participation. You can withdraw from the group without penalty and without jeopardy at any time. If you have any further questions about this project, please feel free to call Dwight L. Rogers, Ph.D. or Leslie M. Babinski, Ph.D., School of Education, University of North Carolina (UNC) at Chapel Hill. In addition, you may contact the UNC Academic Affairs-Institutional Review Board at any time during this project should you feel your rights have been violated: Academic Affairs Institutional Review Board, David Eckerman, CB # 4100, 300 Bynum Hall.

Please keep one copy of this letter and sign the other copy and return it to us if you are interested in participating in this project.

Sincerely,

Leslie M. Babinski, Ph.D.
Dwight L. Rogers, Ph.D.

Consent Form for
Teacher Support Group

I,_____ , consent to be part of the group
for the new teacher consultation project with facilitators from the University of North Carolina at Chapel Hill. My participation will include attending meetings, completing questionnaires, allowing sessions to be audiotaped, and providing written and verbal feedback on this group. I understand that the information discussed will be kept confidential.

_____   _____

Signature   Date

Consent Form for
New Teacher Group Facilitators

Dear New Teacher Group Facilitator,

The group facilitator meetings will provide a forum for the four or five new teacher group facilitators to discuss issues and problems that they encounter during their biweekly meetings with beginning elementary teachers. These sessions will help facilitators consider alternative means to structure and lead the discussions in their new teacher meetings. In addition, the principal facilitators of the group, Dwight L. Rogers and Leslie M. Babinski, will be using information from this group to examine issues important to new facilitators and to the process of group support.

Your participation in this project is voluntary and includes biweekly two-hour facilitator group meetings from September through June for a total of approximately sixteen sessions. We will audio-tape the meetings and we will also be taking notes to document the types of issues that are discussed. We will ask you to provide both verbal and written feedback evaluating the group as a means of support for new teachers. In addition, you will be asked to complete a questionnaire about the group environment in September and June. When we transcribe the tapes, you will be identified only by a code name and the tapes will be kept in a locked file drawer until they are destroyed in two years when the project is completed. Furthermore, when we write about and report on the results of this group, we will not reveal your names, the names of your schools, or any of the names of the students that you mention in the group. In other words, the information collected during the group sessions will remain confidential.

The information you provide may be helpful in determining ways to provide support for new teacher group facilitators in the future. You may also benefit personally from the group through your participation. You can withdraw from the group without penalty and without jeopardy at any time. If you have any further questions about this project, please feel free to call Dwight L. Rogers, Ph.D. or Leslie M. Babinski, Ph.D., School of Education, University of North Carolina (UNC) at Chapel Hill. In addition, you may contact the UNC Academic Affairs-Institutional Review Board at any time during this project should you feel your rights have been violated: Academic Affairs Institutional Review Board, David Eckerman, CB # 4100, 300 Bynum Hall.

Please keep one copy of this letter and sign the other copy and return it to us if you are interested in participating in this project.

Sincerely,

Leslie M. Babinski, Ph.D.
Dwight L. Rogers, Ph.D.

Consent Form for New
Teacher Group Facilitators

I,_____ , consent to be part of the facilitators group for the new teacher consultation project from the University of North Carolina at Chapel Hill. My participation will include attending meetings, completing questionnaires, allowing sessions to be audiotaped, and providing written and verbal feedback on this group. I understand that the information discussed will be kept confidential.

_____   _____

Signature   Date

Appendix D

Code:_____

Interviews for New Teacher Groups

1. When did you decide to become a teacher? What early experiences influence what and how you teach?

2. How would you describe yourself as a teacher?

3. Describe your university teacher education. What did and what didn't it prepare you for?

4. Is teaching what you expected? Please explain.

5. Talk about any colleagues or mentors that you believe were helpful to you as a first-year teacher. How did they play a role in your development as a teacher?

6. How have you changed as a teacher and as a person over the course of this year?

7. What have been your successes this past year?

8. What are the central ideas about education that guide your work? How have they changed over this year? How have they changed since you were an undergraduate?

9. Draw a time line of critical personal events and those related to teaching, both good and bad, which occurred over the course of this year. How did you deal with them? How did they affect your teaching and the way you think about teaching? What, if any, role did the group play in helping you work out some of these issues?

10. Why did you show up for the group week after week?

11. What impact, if any, did the group have on your teaching or on your life as a teacher?

12. Specifically, what about the group was most helpful to you? Least

helpful? What specific session or topic was most relevant for you? Least relevant? Why?

13. In some groups the teachers talked about the state's new accountability plan with an emphasis on end-of-grade testing. Did this accountability plan impact your teaching this year? In what way?

14. What suggestions do you have to make this kind of group more helpful and relevant to beginning teachers? What other suggestions in addition to a new teacher group do you have to help first-year teachers? What about for second- and third-year teachers?

15. What did you like and not like about our roles as facilitators of the group? What suggestions do you have for us?

16. If you were interviewing the other teachers in the group, what additional questions would you ask them? Any questions for me?

17. What other things were important or problematic to you about the group that we haven't talked about?

Appendix E

Starting Your Own New Teacher Group

Over the past few years, we have learned many lessons from our experiences working with new teachers. In this appendix, we offer some guidelines for planning, designing, and implementing problem-based discussion groups for new teachers. Our hope is that by outlining our work with the New Teacher Groups others can modify and adapt our practices to fit the needs of these teachers in their schools.

First we will provide suggestions for (a) planning and logistics, (b) establishing a trusting atmosphere, (c) providing a structure for the group meetings, (d) engaging in the problem-solving process, (e) considering other factors when planning groups for beginning teachers, (f) training facilitators, (g) providing support for the facilitators, and (h) developing your first group meeting. Next, we briefly describe our training module for group facilitators including how we provided supervision and support for the facilitators throughout the year. Finally, we present an outline for things to consider during the first meeting.

Planning and logistics. Before implementing a new teacher discussion group, it is important to determine the other types of support services available for beginning teachers in your school district. In our state, school systems are required to provide a mentor-teacher for all first-year teachers and some offer additional workshops and other support activities. In recognizing that any new service does not operate in a vacuum, it is necessary to obtain the support and sanction of school administrators, principals, and staff developers for your program. It is helpful if new teachers are able to earn continuing education credits for their participation in these groups. Publicize the program and alert all new teachers of the availability of these teacher groups. As university faculty and graduate students, we have found that attending the district's new teacher orientation program is an effective way to inform teachers about the consultation groups. After the groups are formed, allow the participating teachers to determine the meeting places and times that best fit their schedules.

Establishing a trusting atmosphere. It is essential that the group facilitators pay careful attention to establishing the culture of the group. The creation of a safe, comfortable, trusting atmosphere is required to facilitate the group process. Confidentiality and its limits should be discussed at the first meeting. The nonevaluative aspect of the groups is important and it should be emphasized that the consultant will not be evaluating the teachers' competence nor will reports be made to school administrators regarding the discussions in the group. A co-equal, collaborative relationship should be established between group members and facilitators. The fact that all group members were new to teaching helped to establish a safe environment for sharing concerns. The teachers also mentioned the confidential nature of the group, and the fact that teachers were from different schools, contributed to the feeling of the group as a safe place to discuss concerns. The teachers noted that the nonevaluative role of the facilitators was essential in maintaining the confidentiality in the groups and creating a comfortable, nonthreatening atmosphere. This is one reason why school psychologists and counselors are in a good position to offer new teacher consultation groups—they rarely have a direct supervisory relationship with teachers and are thus able to maintain confidentiality. Other district-level personnel without supervisory responsibilities, such as curriculum specialists, could also be trained to facilitate consultation groups.

To encourage teachers to feel comfortable in the groups we have found that sharing success stories, especially during the early meetings of the group, helps to establish trust and to provide an opportunity for teachers to demonstrate their competence. Also, encouraging the judicious use of humor can diffuse stress and contribute to rapport building. Emphasize the importance of consistent group attendance and encourage teachers to be supportive of each other. Beginning teachers are very concerned about time commitments outside of school, so it is important to remind them that there is no "homework" or preparation necessary for group attendance.

Providing a structure for the group meetings. The group meetings focus on discussions around problems and concerns described by one or more participants. Problem-based interactions allow each beginning teacher to share issues and concerns with the entire group. The group, guided by a facilitator, seeks to help the teacher better understand and resolve the problem. As noted earlier, the group facilitators use the following structure to guide the meetings to encourage group problem-solving (see Figure 1).

- A teacher presents his or her problem to the group.

- The facilitator and group members help the teacher better define the problem and develop alternative perspectives as the group seeks to clarify the problem.

- Once the problem or issue is clarified, the group generates possible solutions and derives an initial plan of action for dealing with the problem.

- At later meetings the teacher reports on her follow-up activities— thereby allowing the problem and plan further exploration and collaborative assistance from the group members.

Group facilitators may find it challenging to ensure that each teacher has the opportunity to share his or her problems in an equitable manner.

Although each group is unique, the facilitators for our New Teacher Groups have addressed this issue of fairness by having two or three of the teachers alternate sharing their problem for any one particular meeting. A typical hour-and-a-half or two-hour meeting might look like the following:

- All teachers briefly share with the others what went well and/or did not go so well for them during the previous week (15 minutes).

- The teachers whose problems were discussed at the last meeting report back to the group (10-20 minutes).

- Two or three teachers volunteer to present their problems to discuss with the group (2 minutes).

- The group engages in the problem-solving process focusing on the problems presented by two or three teachers (20—30 minutes for each teacher).

- All of the teachers in the group write brief comments providing their evaluation of the meeting (5 minutes).

Individual meetings may differ, however, and the facilitators must learn to "read" each particular occasion and to be flexible and responsive in order to address current and pressing needs of the teachers. There are times when the problem-solving structure can become too confining, leading facilitators to be open to meeting the expressed needs of their groups at a specific meeting. For instance, sometimes an entire group meeting might be devoted to assisting one teacher. There are even some meetings where very little problem-solving occurs because the teachers need to spend more time on simply sharing both positive and negative school experiences. There is, however, a fine line between a gripe session and the opportunity for teachers to truly express their problems and gain assistance from the group. In general, we have found that this problem-solving format is a powerful and productive way to guide a group discussion so that each participant has an opportunity to present a problem and to receive help from others.

Engaging in the problem-solving process. The role of the group facilitators is to encourage thoughtful dialogue regarding a new teacher's problem or concern. The most difficult task for facilitators is helping the new teachers in the group learn to ask questions that encourage the presenting teachers to more clearly define their problems. Early in the year new teachers are much more eager to provide their colleagues with solutions than ask questions that help them gain a deeper understanding of the context and the complexity of their problems. We have learned that with the guidance and modeling of the facilitators, in time, teachers become better listeners, better questioners, and more thoughtful in their approach to defining a problem before they begin making suggestions. We found that it was helpful to explicitly state the problem-solving model that served as the basis for our discussions. Showing the teachers the problem-solving diagram (see Figure 1) and providing examples gave them a framework for what to expect during the group discussions, as suggested by Zins (1993). The group facilitator should model effective problem solving by asking clarifying questions rather than by primarily offering advice or solutions. It may take some time for the other teachers to see the value in helping the presenting teacher think through the problem before offering solutions. The example provided by the facilitator and gentle guiding of the discussion will help the group members engage in the problem-solving process. Following a mental health consultative model, the teacher should be responsible for outlining a plan for implementation and follow-up. The teachers also mentioned the structure of the groups, the timeliness (help when you need it), and consistency of the meetings as important. One teacher described the group as "flexible, relaxed, yet with a predictable format." Others said that meeting consistently every two weeks helped them know what to expect and that because the agenda was always generated from the participants, that the discussions were always relevant to their lives as beginning teachers. Finally, formative group evaluations should be conducted with an opportunity for the teachers to provide feedback on the group process.

Considering other factors when planning groups for beginning teachers. Group meetings may become more successful by attending to certain factors. Refreshments at each meeting encourages collegiality, rotating the location provides new teachers with varying work settings, and a nonevaluative facilitator is essential for leading the group. We learned not to underestimate the importance of refreshments, after a meeting when one teacher forgot to bring the snacks. After that incident, the host-teacher was always responsible for making this provision. Holding the meetings in the teachers' classrooms also appears to be an important aspect of a group's success. The host teacher often takes the others on a tour of the room—showing them materials, activities, and students' projects. Group members really enjoy seeing the physical organization and instructional arrangements of their colleagues' classrooms.

The new teachers were never evaluated at any time during our New Teacher Group meetings. We believe that this is crucial in order to encourage honest, thoughtful group discussions, and for the teachers to genuinely deal with issues of real concern to them. In order for this type of group to succeed in helping new teachers, participants must feel free to talk about sensitive issues related to their colleagues, children, parents, and administrators in their respective schools. The inclusion of an evaluator, or even an evaluative atmosphere, within the group would sabotage the group process. In fact, having other new teachers from the same school can be a deterrent to dialogue. The most successful groups appear to be those where the teachers are from different schools and even from different school districts. Although we have only had university faculty or graduate students facilitating our groups, we believe that teachers and retired teachers, school counselors, school psychologists, and even central office staff could act as group facilitators, as long as they were in a nonevaluative position in regard to the new teachers.

Training facilitators. The model we followed included two facilitators for each group. Because we are based at a university, we trained graduate students to serve as group facilitators. For each group, one of the facilitators had a teaching background and one had a background in school psychology. This interdisciplinary model worked well. As we just mentioned, there are certainly many different kinds of educational professionals who could be trained to be effective group facilitators for new teacher groups. However, we believe that it is essential for whomever is selected to facilitate the groups to have the following qualities: (a) the ability to actively attend to others' stories, (b) the ability to manage group dynamics, and (c) an open mind regarding approaches to working with new teachers. Flexibility and the ability to see problems from multiple perspectives are also important skills for New Teacher Group facilitators. Our training sequence involves three initial two-hour sessions to orient the facilitators to the consultee-centered consultation model and to the problem-solving process we use in the group. These are the main points we try to communicate to the facilitators in the initial training sessions:

- You don't need to solve the teachers' problems. Giving advice is easy but not very effective. Empowering the teachers takes more time, but is likely to result in a more powerful, longer-lasting effect on the teacher.

- Facilitators must create a trusting, caring atmosphere in the group based on mutual response and genuine warmth and caring.

- The most difficult step in the problem-solving process involves helping the teachers refine or reframe the problem. It is tempting to think that the initial presentation of the problem is the true issue understood in its entirety. In fact, most people gain insight and a better understanding of their problem through the process of verbalization.

In the third training session, transcripts from actual group meetings are read aloud and discussed by the facilitators. By demonstrating the process in action, we hope to provide the facilitators with a deeper understanding of the problem-solving process within the group.

Providing support for the facilitators. In addition to the training sessions for the facilitators before the groups begin, we also conduct biweekly facilitators' meetings that mirror the structure of the New Teacher Group meetings. The format for the facilitators meetings is as follows. Each facilitator takes a turn providing a general update about group(s). Then, each facilitator indicates whether he or she has an issue to present and discuss. The types of issues presented by the facilitators ranged from concerns about group dynamics, to discussions of challenging cases presented by teachers, to issues of confidentiality and countertransference. In these meetings we provide a forum for the group facilitators to reflect on their leadership of the group, to think about alternative ways of addressing their issues, and making plans to implement the ideas in their group meetings. We try to use the same problem-solving approach that is used in the New Teacher Group meetings with the facilitators. This provides the facilitators with an opportunity to see the process modeled and to experience the role of the consultee, that is, the one who is seeking the assistance. We have found that the facilitators appreciate the chance to debrief and talk about the functioning of their group.

There are many layers to promoting problem solving and reflection in a supportive community of learners. The facilitators need a chance to verbalize their concerns with others who are experiencing similar things. In turn, they need an opportunity for reflection and problem solving about how to approach working with their group. The support afforded by the facilitators' meeting may be even more important for people who are facilitating a group alone because they do not have anyone to talk to about the workings of their group.

In the final section we provide an outline of suggestions to consider when organizing and leading the first group meeting.

Developing your first group meeting. The following is an outline that we provided the facilitators to use as a guide for their first New Teacher Group meeting:

Preparation for the meeting:

- Arrange chairs in a circle so that everyone can see everyone else.

- Ask teachers to fill out name tags with names, schools, and grades.

- Provide snacks!

Format for meeting:

1. Welcome everyone and thank them for coming.

2. Ask each teacher to introduce him or herself

3. Provide a brief overview of teacher groups.

 - In the problem-solving group, which is focused on the needs of teachers in the group, there is a chance to talk about problems encountered as a beginning teacher.

 - Discuss meeting day and time, location for meetings, directions to each school, and decide who brings snacks.

 - Exchange phone numbers; pass out sheets.

4. Discuss the necessity and importance of maintaining strict confidentiality for everyone participating in the group.

5. Ask each teacher to say one thing that has gone really well for them this school year and one thing that they find challenging or frustrating.

6. Describe the problem-solving approach briefly; use examples of issues teachers mentioned during sharing, if possible.

7. Schedule the next several meetings; be sure to work around teacher-parent meetings and other teacher commitments.

8. In closing, answer questions, remind everyone of the next meeting, and thank them for coming.

Figure 1

Illustration of the Problem-Solving Process in the New Teacher Consultation Groups

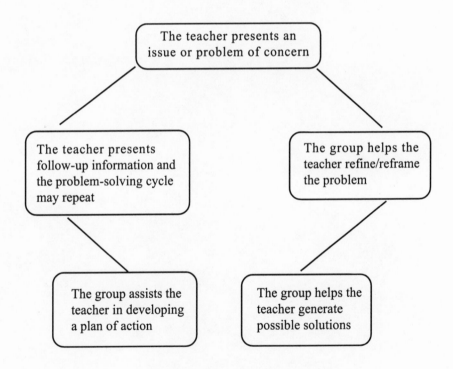

The teacher presents an issue or problem of concern

The teacher presents follow-up information and the problem-solving cycle may repeat

The group helps the teacher refine/reframe the problem

The group assists the teacher in developing a plan of action

The group helps the teacher generate possible solutions

Subject Index

129

Author Index